WORKBOOK PLUS
TCAP PRACTICE
GRADE 3

HOUGHTON MIFFLIN HARCOURT

Illustrations

Elizabeth Allen: 91, 93, 101, 109, 111, 115; **Winifred Barnum-Newman:** 85; **Burgandy Beam:** 124, 131; **Linda Howard Bittner:** 45; **Donna Catanese:** 118; **Eldon Doty:** 27, 59; **Larry Frederick:** 55; **Patti Goodnow:** 60; **April Hartmann:** 22; **Seitu Hayden:** 2, 41; **Jean Helmer:** 113; **Reggie Holladay:** 129, 138; **Toni Hormann:** 73; **CD Hullinger:** 64; **Tim Jones:** 32; **Victor Kennedy:** 51, 74; **Gary Krejca:** 20, 43, 87; **Dean Lindberg:** 83, 147; **Richard Lo:** 105; **Ginna Magee:** 62, 88, 99; **Robert Masheris:** 17, 31, 117, 130, 150; **Tom McKee:** 1, 10, 70, 135; **Dawn Marie Pavlowski:** 26, 141; **Bill Petersen:** 6, 35, 78, 81, 148; **Phyllis Pollema-Cahill:** 19, 72, 125; **Wendy Rasmussen:** 37, 53, 120, 139; **Bart Rivers:** 97; **Doug Roy:** 30, 34; **Slug Signorino:** 68, **Stan Tusan:** 90; **George Ulrich:** 8, 14, 39

Printed in the U.S.A.

ISBN-13: 978-0-547-32974-1
ISBN-10: 0-547-32974-1

16 -0928- 16 15
4500523900

Table of Contents • Workbook Plus

Part 2
Writing, Listening, Speaking, and Viewing

Table of Contents • TCAP Practice

Daily Practice Tests

WORKBOOK PLUS

Name _____

1 What Is a Sentence?

Sentences	The very first cars looked strange. People laughed at them.
Not sentences	The very first cars. Laughed at them.

A Read the two groups of words after each number. Underline the group of words that is a sentence.

1. The first automobiles amazed people.

   Rode on horses or bicycles.

2. A strange sight on the roads.

   Very few people had cars.

3. Inventors from different countries.

   Some cars had steam engines.

4. The Stanley twins built a steam car.

   The most famous of all the steam automobiles.

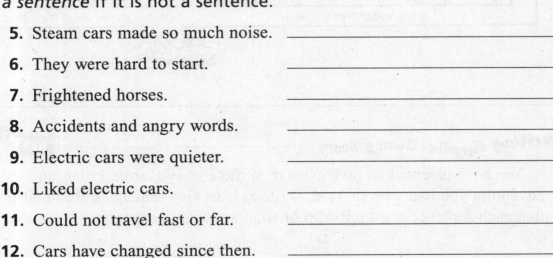

B Write *sentence* if the group of words is a sentence. Write *not a sentence* if it is not a sentence.

5. Steam cars made so much noise. _____

6. They were hard to start. _____

7. Frightened horses. _____

8. Accidents and angry words. _____

9. Electric cars were quieter. _____

10. Liked electric cars. _____

11. Could not travel fast or far. _____

12. Cars have changed since then. _____

(continued)

Grade 3: Unit 1 The Sentence *(Use with pupil book pages 32–33.)*
  Skill: Students will identify sentences.

**WORKBOOK PLUS
TCAP PRACTICE**

1

Name _____

1 What Is a Sentence? *(continued from page 1)*

Challenge

Drive the car to the garage. Only take roads with groups of words that are sentences.

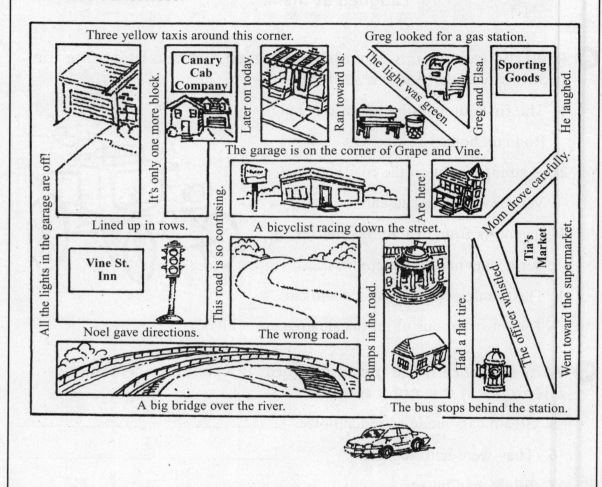

Three yellow taxis around this corner.

Greg looked for a gas station.

Canary Cab Company

Later on today.

Ran toward us.

The light was green.

Greg and Elsa.

Sporting Goods

He laughed.

It's only one more block.

All the lights in the garage are off!

The garage is on the corner of Grape and Vine.

Are here!

Mom drove carefully.

Lined up in rows.

This road is so confusing.

A bicyclist racing down the street.

Tia's Market

Vine St. Inn

Noel gave directions.

The wrong road.

Bumps in the road.

Had a flat tire.

The officer whistled.

Went toward the supermarket.

A big bridge over the river.

The bus stops behind the station.

Writing Application: A Story

NARRATING

You have invented an invisible car. Write a story that describes an adventure you had with this car. Write at least five sentences. Remember that each sentence must tell who or what and what happened.

Grade 3: Unit 1 The Sentence *(Use with pupil book pages 32–33.)*
Skill: Students will identify and will write sentences.

Name _____

Writing Good Sentences

A complete sentence and an incomplete one	Pyramids are tall. And very big.
Complete sentence	Pyramids are tall and very big.

Writing Complete Sentences 1–5. Fix each incomplete sentence from a report by adding it to a complete sentence. Rewrite the paragraph, making the changes.

Revising

The ancient Egyptians built many pyramids. Pyramids were giant tombs. Used to bury Egyptian kings. The kings were buried with things they used every day. Egyptians believed. In life after death.

Egyptian pyramids were built of heavy stones. Or bricks. The stones were so huge that the workers needed boats to carry them. The pyramids were built near the Nile River. Workers had to be careful. Not to let the great stones drop. A single stone. Could crush hundreds of people.

_____

_____

_____

_____

_____

_____

_____

_____

_____

_____

_____

(continued)

Grade 3: Unit 1   The Sentence   *(Use with pupil book pages 34–35.)*
   Skill: Students will identify fluence fragments and write complete sentences.

WORKBOOK PLUS TCAP PRACTICE   3

Name _____

Writing Good Sentences (continued from page 3)

Incomplete sentence	Are very large.
Complete sentence	Pyramids are very large.

Writing Complete Sentences 6–10. Fix each incomplete sentence from this book about pyramids by adding a word that tells *who* or *what* or by adding the incomplete sentence to a complete sentence. Write the new sentences on the lines below.

Revising

The ancient Egyptians used water, straw, and rocks to build the pyramids. Was also used for drinking and cooking. It was taken from the Nile River. Straw was dried from the plants that grew in the marshes. Was gathered into bundles and carried to the construction area. Rocks came from the granite stones. That were in the land. Workers dug up the stones. And broke them into rocks. When the builders had all the materials, they would grind the straw and the rocks together. Water was then added to make a thick mixture, like cake batter. Was formed into blocks and then dried in the sun. Then the blocks were used to build the pyramid.

6. _____

_____

7. _____

_____

8. _____

_____

9. _____

_____

10. _____

_____

Grade 3: Unit 1   The Sentence   *(Use with pupil book pages 34–35.)*
Skill: Students will add a subject to complete a sentence fragment or fix incomplete sentences by adding them to complete sentences.

2 Statements and Questions

| Statement | Our country has a birthday. |
| Question | What day is it on? |

A Write *statement* if the sentence tells something. Write *question* if the sentence asks something.

1. Another country ruled our land. _____

2. Many people wanted their freedom. _____

3. Was George Washington one of them? _____

4. Some men wrote an important paper. _____

5. What did that paper say? _____

6. Would our country become free? _____

7. When would our country become free? _____

8. Our new country had 13 states. _____

B 9–14. This story has two missing capital letters and four missing or incorrect end marks. Use proofreading marks to correct each sentence.

Example: our country is very special?.

Proofreading

Proofreading Marks

¶ Indent
∧ Add
⌐ Delete
≡ Capital letter
/ Small letter

Happy Birthday, USA!

Everybody has a birthday Countries have

birthdays too. do you know the birthday of our country It is

celebrated each year on the Fourth of July. on that day in 1776

our leaders told the world we were free? How do you celebrate

that day.

(continued)

2 Statements and Questions (continued from page 5)

Challenge

1. The boy with the flag asks a question. Write the question.

_____

2. The girl wearing boots makes a statement. Write the statement.

_____

3. The girl with the drum asks a question. Write the question.

_____

4. The boy with the horn makes a statement. Write the statement.

_____

5. Does the man tell something or ask something?

_____

6. Write the sentence the man says.

_____

Writing Application: A Letter

INFORMING

Suppose that you have been to a parade on our country's birthday. Write a letter to one of your friends. Write three statements that tell what you did and saw at the parade. Write three questions that you want to ask your friend.

Grade 3: Unit 1   The Sentence   *(Use with pupil book pages 36–37.)*
Skill: Students will write statements and questions.

3 Commands and Exclamations

Command	Pull the fire alarm.
Exclamation	That building is on fire!

A Write *command* if the sentence tells someone to do something. Write *exclamation* if the sentence shows strong feeling.

1. Here come the fire engines!   _____

2. Don't cross the street now.   _____

3. Give them plenty of room.   _____

4. The engines make so much noise!   _____

5. The hook-and-ladder truck is huge!   _____

6. Stay far away from the fire.   _____

7. The smoke is so thick!   _____

B 8–14. This poster for fire safety has four commands and two exclamations. Use proofreading marks to correct the mistakes.

Example: to get help, dial 911 and speak clearly.

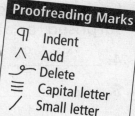

Proofreading Marks

¶	Indent
∧	Add
⌇	Delete
≡	Capital letter
/	Small letter

Proofreading

Stay calm if you are near a fire Try not to run.

listen for directions. Always do what the firefighters

tell you They know what to do in a fire fires are

dangerous. How brave firefighters are Thank goodness

they help us

(continued)

Grade 3: Unit 1   The Sentence   *(Use with pupil book pages 38–39.)*
Skill: Students will identify and will punctuate commands and exclamations.

WORKBOOK PLUS
TCAP PRACTICE   **7**

3 Commands and Exclamations (continued from page 7)

Challenge

Rich wants to put out the campfire, but he doesn't know how. Write three commands to help him.

1. _____

2. _____

3. _____

Look at the picture. Find things that might make Rich feel excited, surprised, or afraid. Write three exclamations that Rich might say.

4. _____

5. _____

6. _____

Writing Application: Instructions

You are a fire chief. You want the engines, hoses, and ladders cleaned. Write three commands that you would put on the firehouse wall, telling the firefighters what to do. Then write three exclamations showing your excitement about the great job the firefighters did.

8 WORKBOOK PLUS
TCAP PRACTICE

Grade 3: Unit 1   The Sentence   (Use with pupil book pages 38–39.)
Skill: Students will write commands and exclamations.

Name _____

4 The Subject of a Sentence

> subject
> |
> **My friend** has a package of seeds.
>
> subject
> |
> **She** has a package of seeds.

Write each sentence. Then underline the subject.

1. Our class does an experiment for science.

_____

2. We plant two bean seeds in different pots.

_____

3. One pot gets no water.

_____

4. Gary waters the other plant every day.

_____

5. Leah checks the pot with the watered seed.

_____

6. She sees a tiny bean plant.

_____

7. Rico checks the unwatered pot.

_____

8. He sees no plant at all.

_____

9. Mrs. West explains the experiment.

_____

10. Water helps seeds grow.

_____

(continued)

Grade 3: Unit 1   The Sentence   *(Use with pupil book pages 40–41.)*
   Skill: Students will identify the subjects of sentences.

WORKBOOK PLUS
TCAP PRACTICE
9

4 The Subject of a Sentence (continued from page 9)

Challenge

Count the flowers in front of each sentence. Write a subject with that number of words to complete the sentence.

1. _____ grows in a garden.

2. _____ do experiments.

3. _____
   _____ need more water.

4. _____
   _____ plant seeds.

5. _____
   _____ eat vegetables.

Writing Application: A Science Report

Suppose that you are a scientist. You are doing an experiment to see if music helps plants grow. Write four sentences about your experiment. Give each sentence a different subject.

10 **WORKBOOK PLUS**
TCAP PRACTICE

Grade 3: Unit 1 The Sentence *(Use with pupil book pages 40–41.)*
Skill: Students will identify and will write the subjects of sentences.

5 The Predicate of a Sentence

Subject	Predicate
This book	tells about jobs.

Write each sentence. Then underline the predicate.

1. Many people work with animals.

_____

2. Arlo works in a zoo.

_____

3. He feeds the elephants every morning.

_____

4. The monkeys play silly tricks on him.

_____

5. The other workers laugh.

_____

6. Maria is a special doctor.

_____

7. She helps many animals.

_____

8. Jeanette likes animals.

_____

9. She owns a pet store.

_____

10. All of her birds sing happily.

_____

(continued)

Grade 3: Unit 1   The Sentence   *(Use with pupil book pages 42–43.)*
Skill: Students will identify the predicates of sentences.

WORKBOOK PLUS
TCAP PRACTICE   11

Name _____

5 The Predicate of a Sentence (continued from page 11)

Challenge

Underline the predicate of each sentence. Then write the first letter of the first word of each predicate. The letters will spell the name of the animal that each poem tells about.

1. This animal pushes over its feed pail.

It is muddy from its head to its tail.

It grunts happily from behind the wooden rail. _____

2. It dives into the clear, cool pond.

It uses its paddles very well.

This bird crosses quickly to the shore beyond.

It knows the sound of the farmer's dinner bell. _____

3. A girl sees an animal.

She hears a funny sound.

This animal enjoys its dinner of grass.

It eats everything on the ground.

It plods lazily around and around. _____

4. This tiny animal makes a noisy squeak.

We open the barn door for a sneaky peek.

The furry thing uses its sense of smell.

It senses danger only too well.

I enjoy this game of hide-and-seek. _____

Writing Application: A Journal
DESCRIBING

Suppose that you train dogs, horses, and elephants to do tricks for a circus. Write four sentences in your journal, describing what you taught the animals today. Use a different predicate in each sentence.

Grade 3: Unit 1   The Sentence   *(Use with pupil book pages 42–43.)*
Skill: Students will identify and will write the predicates of sentences.

6 Correcting Run-on Sentences

Wrong	We use numbers every day they are everywhere. Numbers are helpful could we do without them?
Right	We use numbers every day. They are everywhere. Numbers are helpful. Could we do without them?

A Correct each run-on sentence. Use capital letters and end marks correctly.

1. We like arithmetic numbers are fun.

   _____

2. Beth adds many numbers her answers are usually right.

   _____

3. Hans divides quickly he finishes first in the class.

   _____

B 4–8. This story has five run-on sentences. Use proofreading marks to correct each run-on sentence.

Example: Some people can count very well. others sometimes
have trouble.

Proofreading Marks	
¶	Indent
∧	Add
ℐ	Delete
≡	Capital letter
/	Small letter

Mrs. Muddle

Mrs. Muddle is very mixed up she does

not know numbers or arithmetic. How many children

does she have she doesn't know. Where does she live she

can't tell you. What is her phone number nobody knows. How

old is she? She doesn't know. Learn your numbers then this

won't happen to you.

(continued)

Grade 3: Unit 1   The Sentence   *(Use with pupil book pages 44–45.)*
Skill: Students will identify and will correct run-on sentences.

**WORKBOOK PLUS
TCAP PRACTICE**   **13**

Name _____

6 Correcting Run-on Sentences (continued from page 13)

Challenge

There is a secret message in these sentences. Find the run-on sentences, and fix them with a red pencil or marker. Write capital letters and end marks where they belong.

Today our class learned about shapes next week we will learn more. This shape has three sides it is called a triangle. What shape is this can you tell me? How many sides does a square have each square has four sides. Our teacher told us something what did she say? A circle is round other shapes are not round. What is a rectangle rectangles have four sides. We looked at pictures of kites kites have different shapes.

Write the red capital letters on the line. They spell a secret message for you.

Secret Message: _____

Writing Application: A Math Problem — CREATING

You are a writer. You are writing a third grade math book. Write a word problem that is at least four sentences long. Be careful not to write any run-on sentences.

Grade 3: Unit 1 The Sentence (*Use with pupil book pages 44–45.*)
Skill: Students will identify and will correct run-on sentences.

Name _____

Writing Good Sentences

| Run-on sentence | The South Pole is cold it is snowy. |
| Correct sentence | The South Pole is cold, and it is snowy. |

Fixing Run-on Sentences 1–5. Fix each run-on sentence from this report by adding a comma *(,)* and the word *and*.

Revising

    The Arctic is solid it looks like frozen land. Now we know the Arctic is really frozen water. People live in some parts of the Arctic they grow food there. It is not as cold as you might think. In the summer, you can get a sunburn!

    The South Pole is too cold for living things only scientists spend time there. They wear many layers of clothes they wear boots filled with air. The wind blows snow around people can get buried in minutes.

1. _____

_____

2. _____

_____

3. _____

_____

4. _____

_____

5. _____

_____

(continued)

Grade 3: Unit 1 The Sentence *(Use with pupil book pages 46–47.)*
Skill: Students will correct run-on sentences.

WORKBOOK PLUS
TCAP PRACTICE
15

Name _____

Writing Good Sentences (continued from page 15)

Short sentences	It was hard to reach the North Pole. Some explorers made it.
Combined sentence	It was hard to reach the North Pole, but some explorers made it.

Combining Sentences 6–10. Combine each underlined pair of sentences from this book about the North Pole by adding a comma *(,)* and the word *and, but,* or *or.*

Revising

The North Pole is covered with ice. Traveling on ice is difficult. The ice chunks crash against each other. They crush anything in their path. Only dog teams can travel across the frozen sea. This is how explorers traveled. They had to carry extra food. They would run out. Many explorers starved.

Robert Peary and Matthew Henson reached the North Pole in 1909. Peary was going to reach the Pole. He was going to die trying. Henson and Peary were brave men. They earned a place in history.

6. _____

_____

7. _____

_____

8. _____

_____

9. _____

_____

10. _____

_____

Grade 3: Unit 1 The Sentence *(Use with pupil book pages 46–47.)*
Skill: Students will combine short sentences with *and, but,* or *or.*

1 What Are Nouns?

> person   things   place
> My **uncle** has **cows** on his **farm**.

Write the two nouns in each sentence.

1. A farmer plants corn. _____

2. His daughter works in the field. _____

3. The tractor rolls over the ground. _____

4. The seeds go into the soil. _____

5. The girl walks down the rows. _____

6. Sun and rain are helpful. _____

7. Soon the plants are as tall as a person. _____

8. A big machine comes onto the land. _____

9. Many helpers pick the crops. _____

10. Workers load the heavy boxes. _____

11. Now the truck is full of vegetables. _____

12. The driver leaves the farm. _____

13. Some potatoes are sent to stores. _____

14. Carrots and peas go too. _____

15. People will buy the food. _____

16. Some trucks stop at roadside markets. _____

17. Farmers can lose money easily. _____

18. Crops can be damaged by bad weather. _____

19. My uncle loves his farm. _____

20. There is always work to do on the farm. _____

(continued)

Grade 3: Unit 2 Nouns *(Use with pupil book pages 60–61.)*
Skill: Students will identify and will write nouns.

**WORKBOOK PLUS
TCAP PRACTICE**   **17**

Name _____

1 What Are Nouns? *(continued from page 17)*

Challenge

Write a noun to finish each rhyme. The rhymes tell about people, places, and things on a farm.

1. I am a person.

My name rhymes with *look*.

I make corn for dinner.

I am a _____.

2. I am a place.

My name rhymes with *rake*.

People swim here.

I am a _____.

3. I am a thing.

My name rhymes with *eat*.

I grow in the garden.

I am a _____.

4. I am a place.

My name rhymes with *rest*.

A hen lays its eggs here.

I am a _____.

5. We are people.

Our name rhymes with *ten*.

We are not women.

We are _____.

6. I am a place.

My name rhymes with *hard*.

I have green grass.

I am a _____.

7. I am a thing.

My name rhymes with *now*.

I give people milk.

I am a _____.

8. I am a person.

My name rhymes with *fun*.

I am the farmer's child.

I am a _____.

Now write two rhymes of your own on another piece of paper. Write about a noun that names a person, a place, or a thing.

Writing Application: A News Report

DESCRIBING

Suppose that you are a TV news reporter. A giant talking vegetable has just been discovered. Write a news report, describing the vegetable and where it was found. Use nouns that name people, places, and things.

18 WORKBOOK PLUS
TCAP PRACTICE

Grade 3: Unit 2   Nouns   *(Use with pupil book pages 60–61.)*
Skill: Students will write nouns.

2 Common and Proper Nouns

common noun   common noun

A **nurse** works at a **hospital**.

proper noun   proper noun

Carol Pike works at **Northside Hospital**.

A   Write *common noun* or *proper noun* for each underlined noun.

1. <u>Clara Barton</u> helped people all her life. _____

2. She was a nurse during the <u>Civil War</u>. _____

3. Miss Barton took care of many <u>soldiers</u>. _____

4. She worked for the <u>Red Cross</u> in other lands. _____

5. Clara began a Red Cross in the <u>United States</u>. _____

6. The Red Cross can help people after a <u>storm</u>. _____

7. Little City had a bad flood last <u>March</u>. _____

B   **8–12.** Use proofreading marks to correct the two common nouns and three proper nouns in this report.

Example: Nurses work in H̲ospitals and in clinics.

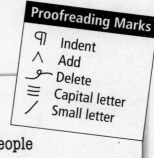

Proofreading Marks

¶   Indent
∧   Add
⌐   Delete
≡   Capital letter
/   Small letter

Proofreading

       Today the red cross still helps in an

emergency. Nurses like chris daniels take care of people

who are hurt. Other workers bring Supplies where they are

needed. These workers help all around the united states.

They help around the World too.

(continued)

Grade 3: Unit 2   Nouns   *(Use with pupil book pages 62–63.)*
Skill: Students will identify and will use common and proper nouns.

WORKBOOK PLUS
TCAP PRACTICE   **19**

2 Common and Proper Nouns (continued from page 19)

Challenge

The picture below shows a part of Little City. Look at the numbered items in the picture. Then complete the chart below. Write a proper noun to match each common noun. The numbers on the drawing match the numbers on the chart.

Little City

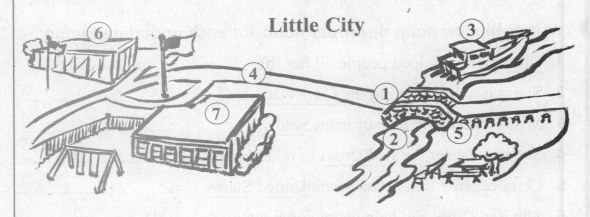

COMMON NOUNS	PROPER NOUNS
1. bridge	1. **Rainbow Bridge**
2. river	2. _____
3. boat	3. _____
4. road	4. _____
5. park	5. _____
6. library	6. _____
7. school	7. _____

Writing Application: A Letter

Suppose that you work for the Red Cross. You are helping people who have left their homes because of a flood. Write a letter to a friend, describing your work. Include common and proper nouns.

20 WORKBOOK PLUS
TCAP PRACTICE

Grade 3: Unit 2 Nouns *(Use with pupil book pages 62–63.)*
Skill: Students will write common and proper nouns.

Name _____

3 Nouns in the Subject

| Subject | Cold **weather** brings snow and ice. |
| Subject | **Ella Grotz** loves winter storms. |

Write the noun in the subject of each sentence.

1. A blizzard is not just snow. _____

2. Very strong winds blow in a blizzard. _____

3. Snow flies all around. _____

4. Tall trees bend in the wind. _____

5. Oaktown is having a blizzard. _____

6. Franklin Street is covered with snow. _____

7. Some cars are stuck on a hill. _____

8. All the squirrels hide in their nests. _____

9. Most people stay in their warm houses. _____

10. Ella Grotz puts on her boots. _____

11. Her heavy jacket will keep her warm. _____

12. The big plow is ready to go. _____

13. Mrs. Grotz drives the plow. _____

14. Al is her helper. _____

15. A yellow truck follows the plow. _____

16. Salt is put on the streets. _____

17. The ice melts into water. _____

18. Then drivers move easily on the streets. _____

19. Sometimes even the plows get stuck! _____

20. Schools sometimes close in blizzards. _____

21. More police officers watch the traffic. _____

22. A city needs good workers in a blizzard. _____

(continued)

Grade 3: Unit 2   Nouns   *(Use with pupil book pages 64–65.)*
Skill: Students will identify nouns in the subjects of sentences.

WORKBOOK PLUS
TCAP PRACTICE

21

Name _____

3 Nouns in the Subject (continued from page 21)

Challenge ⭐

Read each sentence below. Find and circle a noun in the puzzle to complete each sentence. Write the noun in the sentence. The words in the puzzle may run from left to right or from top to bottom.

```
S   S R J A C K N
L   N A F H I N
E   S N O W B F R
D   T U V K O O
S   H A T S O R
C   A R R O T T
B   O Y S H S K
```

1. _____ is a winter month.

2. _____ makes everything white and sparkling.

3. Woolly _____ warm our heads in winter.

4. We left an orange _____ for the rabbit.

5. Many _____ and girls enjoy winter sports.

6. Shiny _____ line up for the race.

7. _____ keep our feet warm and dry.

8. _____ _____ visits only during winter.

Now choose four of the nouns that you circled. On another piece of paper, write four sentences, using each noun as the subject of a sentence.

Writing Application: A Journal ——————— EXPRESSING

You have been snowed in by a blizzard. You have no electricity because of the storm. Write five sentences about this day. Underline the noun in the subject of each sentence.

Grade 3: Unit 2 Nouns (Use with pupil book pages 64–65.)
Skill: Students will identify and will write nouns in the subjects of sentences.

Writing with Nouns

Without elaboration	The Vietnamese New Year lasts for three days.
With elaboration	The Vietnamese New Year, **called Tet,** lasts for three days.

Elaborating Sentences 1–5. Elaborate each underlined sentence from this book about holidays by adding the words in parentheses.

Revising

Holidays are special times. People celebrate important events. Some holidays mark a new season or honor a person. Other holidays honor history. (like the Fourth of July) Some holidays are celebrated in many countries. (like Christmas) Many holidays celebrate traditions and customs.

Carnival takes place six weeks before Easter. (a special celebration) During Carnival, there are many parades. A very famous Carnival is held in New Orleans. (Mardi Gras) Noruz begins on March 21. (Iranian New Year) The holiday lasts 13 days. On the last day of Noruz, families have picnics.

1. _____

_____

2. _____

_____

3. _____

_____

4. _____

_____

5. _____

_____

(continued)

Grade 3: Unit 2 Nouns *(Use with pupil book pages 66–67.)*
Skill: Students will elaborate sentences by adding nouns.

**WORKBOOK PLUS
TCAP PRACTICE** 23

Writing with Nouns (continued from page 23)

Not combined	Japanese boys have their own holiday. Japanese girls have their own holiday.
Combined	Japanese boys **and girls** have their own holiday.

Combining Sentences 6–10. Combine each pair of underlined sentences from this report. Write the new sentences.

Revising

   Korean Children's Day is celebrated every May 5. School is closed that day. <u>Children often go to museums. Adults often go to museums.</u> They also attend dance shows and sporting events. <u>Boys enter writing contests. Girls enter writing contests.</u>

   The African American holiday Kwanzaa lasts for seven days. Each day of Kwanzaa has a special meaning. <u>Families enjoy a feast. Friends enjoy a feast.</u> <u>Children make small gifts for friends. Parents make small gifts for friends.</u>

   Fiestas are celebrated in Mexico. <u>Saints are honored at fiestas. National heroes are honored at fiestas.</u> People sing, dance, play games, and hold parades.

6. _____

_____

7. _____

_____

8. _____

_____

9. _____

_____

10. _____

_____

Grade 3: Unit 2 Nouns (Use with pupil book pages 66–67.)
Skill: Students will combine sentences with the same predicate.

4 Singular and Plural Nouns

Singular nouns	We saw a **sparrow** in one **field**.
Plural nouns	We saw many **sparrows** in those **fields**.

A Write *singular* or *plural* for each underlined noun.

1. A sparrow is a small <u>bird</u>. _____

2. Sparrows are found in many <u>states</u>. _____

3. A sparrow makes its <u>nest</u> from grass and straw. _____

4. Sparrows also use <u>rags</u> in their nests. _____

5. Soft <u>feathers</u> fill the bottom of the nest. _____

6. A sparrow's <u>egg</u> is tiny. _____

7. A <u>farmer</u> may not like sparrows. _____

8. Sparrows often eat the <u>buds</u> of fruit trees. _____

B 9–15. Use proofreading marks to correct the seven nouns in this paragraph from a diary.

Example: Sammi uses a special pen̷ to write in her diary.

Proofreading

Proofreading Marks	
¶	Indent
∧	Add
୬	Delete
≡	Capital letter
/	Small letter

Dear Diary,

Today at the parks I fed some sparrow. They

ate breadcrumb from my two hand. They chirped a pretty

songs as they ate. I think sparrows are my favorite bird.

I like them even more than bluejay.

(continued)

Grade 3: Unit 2 Nouns *(Use with pupil book pages 68–69.)*
Skill: Students will identify and will write singular and plural nouns.

WORKBOOK PLUS
TCAP PRACTICE
25

Name _____

4 **Singular and Plural Nouns** (continued from page 25)

Challenge

Help the bird return to its nest. The bird can follow only paths that have plural nouns written on them. It must stay off all paths that have singular nouns.

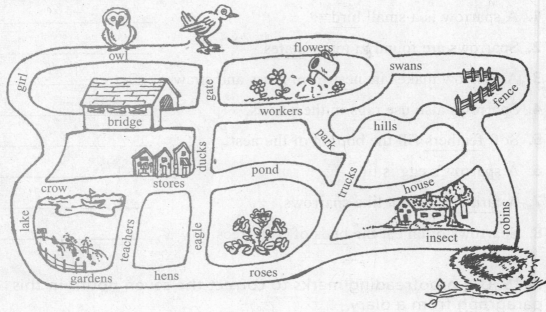

Now write four sentences describing the bird's trip. Underline each singular noun. Circle each plural noun.

_____

_____

_____

_____

Writing Application: Directions ————————————

  You are a sparrow. Write directions to tell another sparrow how to find your nest. Describe trees, rocks, and other things to look for along the way. Use three singular nouns and three plural nouns in your directions.

© Houghton Mifflin Harcourt Publishing Company

Grade 3: Unit 2 Nouns (*Use with pupil book pages 68–69.*)
Skill: Students will identify and will use singular and plural nouns.

Name _____

5 Plural Nouns with -es

Singular nouns	circu_s_	dish	branch	fox
Plural nouns	circus**es**	dish**es**	branch**es**	fox**es**

A Write the plural form of the underlined noun.

1. Ms. Harris came with her <u>toolbox</u>.

Other people brought _____ too.

2. Kira wanted to repair each <u>bench</u>.

Everyone painted and repaired the _____.

3. Marc forgot to clean his <u>brush</u>.

All the other _____ were cleaned.

4. Each worker had a <u>glass</u> of milk.

They put their empty _____ in the kitchen.

Challenge

Write a one-word title for each picture. The title should be a plural noun.

1. _____ **2.** _____ **3.** _____

On another piece of paper, write one sentence about each picture. Include the plural noun you wrote below the picture. Then write a fourth sentence that uses all three plural nouns.

Grade 3: Unit 2 Nouns *(Use with pupil book page 70.)*
Skill: Students will form plural nouns by adding *es*.

WORKBOOK PLUS
TCAP PRACTICE
27

6 More Plural Nouns with -es

Singular nouns	one **copy**	one **hobby**
Plural nouns	two **cop<u>ies</u>**	many **hobb<u>ies</u>**

Write the plural of the noun in parentheses to complete each sentence.

1. Edgar Allan Poe wrote poems and _____. **(story)**

2. He often wrote _____. **(mystery)**

3. Sometimes he wrote about _____. **(family)**

4. Poe even wrote about their _____. **(worry)**

5. He lived in New York and other _____. **(city)**

6. Most _____ have books by Mr. Poe. **(library)**

Challenge

Read the mystery riddle. The answer is written upside down.

Mystery Riddle: We are bigger than dimes.
We are worth less than nickels.
What are we? pennies

Now write three mystery riddles of your own. Write the answer to each riddle upside down. The answer should be the plural form of a noun from the Word Box.

baby	butterfly	puppy	fly	diary	pony

_____

_____

_____

_____

Grade 3: Unit 2 Nouns *(Use with pupil book page 71.)*
Skill: Students will form the plural of nouns ending with a consonant and *y*.

Name _____

7 Special Plural Nouns

Singular	man	woman	child	mouse	tooth	foot	goose
Plural	men	women	children	mice	teeth	feet	geese

Write the plural form of the noun in parentheses to complete each sentence.

1. Many _____ read fairy tales. **(child)**

2. In one tale, a cat wears boots on its _____. **(foot)**

3. Have you read about the cat with sharp _____? **(tooth)**

4. Some furry _____ wanted to put a bell on her. **(mouse)**

5. Did Mother Goose have one goose or many _____? **(goose)**

6. Do men and _____ really ride on birds? **(woman)**

7. I like the tale about the three giant _____. **(man)**

8. Often the youngest _____ fall into the most trouble. **(child)**

9. The stepmothers are often mean _____. **(woman)**

10. Why are fairy tales always full of _____? **(mouse)**

11. The ogre in many tales has big eyes and _____. **(tooth)**

12. What would you call two Mother _____? **(goose)**

13. Do you know the story of the girl with the iron _____? **(foot)**

14. There are usually three _____ in fairy tales. **(child)**

15. Beneath the old fir tree lives a little family of _____. **(mouse)**

16. There are four _____ in the Bremen music group. **(man)**

17. The shoemaker's elves loved little _____. **(child)**

18. Goose Girl had many _____ around her. **(goose)**

19. Did the kittens need mittens for hands or _____? **(foot)**

20. How many _____ filled the tub? **(man)**

(continued)

Grade 3: Unit 2 Nouns *(Use with pupil book pages 72–73.)*
Skill: Students will form and will use irregular plural nouns.

WORKBOOK PLUS
TCAP PRACTICE 29

Name _____

7 Special Plural Nouns (continued from page 29)

Challenge

Complete this crossword puzzle. Write singular and plural nouns to match the picture clues.

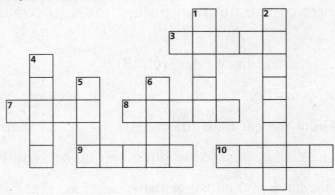

ACROSS

3.

7.

8.

9.

10.

DOWN

1.

2.

4.

5.

6.

Writing Application: A Fairy Tale

NARRATING

Here is the first sentence of a fairy tale. "Once upon a time, there was a frog with flat feet." Add five sentences to this fairy tale. Use the plural forms of four nouns from the Word Box.

| child | man | goose | tooth | mouse | woman |

Grade 3: Unit 2 Nouns *(Use with pupil book pages 72–73.)*
Skill: Students will use singular and plural forms of irregular nouns correctly.

8 Singular Possessive Nouns

Singular Nouns	Singular Possessive Nouns
horse	**horse's** owner
Janet	**Janet's** horse
cow	**cow's** ears

A Write the possessive form of the noun in parentheses to complete the sentence.

1. _____ book has tall tales about Pecos Bill. **(Andy)**

2. Bill was wrapped in a _____ blanket. **(baby)**

3. The little _____ pet was a bear cub. **(boy)**

4. One day Pecos fell off his _____ wagon. **(father)**

5. He grew up in a _____ den. **(coyote)**

6. Later on, _____ horse threw him to the moon. **(Bill)**

7. Amy remembers her _____ stories. **(grandfather)**

8. _____ grandfather was a cowhand. **(Amy)**

B 9–12. Use proofreading marks to correct the four possessive nouns in this e-mail message.

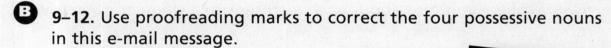

Example: A ~~storytellers~~ storyteller's tall tales are fun to hear.
        ^

Proofreading Marks

¶	Indent
∧	Add
⌐	Delete
≡	Capital letter
/	Small letter

☐ **Proofreading**   **e-mail**

To: Sara
From: Amy
Subject: Stories

I love to hear my grandfathers stories. He tells of Americas legends

of the Old West. He can describe a cowboys adventure. He can also

tell a heros tale. I hope you can come soon to hear some.

(continued)

Grade 3: Unit 2   Nouns   *(Use with pupil book pages 74–75.)*
Skill: Students will form singular possessive nouns.

WORKBOOK PLUS
TCAP PRACTICE   **31**

Name _____

8 Singular Possessive Nouns (continued from page 31)

Challenge

Draw a picture of a person or an animal from the Old West in each empty box below. Then draw something in the box that belongs to that person or animal.

1.

3.

2.

4.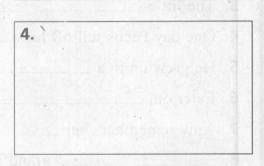

Now write a sentence about each picture. Use a singular possessive noun in each sentence.

1. _____

2. _____

3. _____

4. _____

Writing Application: A Diary

EXPRESSING

    You are a cowhand on a long cattle drive. You have ridden all day with the other cowhands. Write six sentences in your diary, describing your day. Use at least four singular possessive nouns in your sentences.

© Houghton Mifflin Harcourt Publishing Company

32 WORKBOOK PLUS
TCAP PRACTICE

Grade 3: Unit 2 Nouns *(Use with pupil book pages 74–75.)*
Skill: Students will use singular possessive nouns correctly.

9 Plural Possessive Nouns

Plural Nouns	Plural Possessive Nouns
brothers	**brothers'** boats
puppies	**puppies'** toys
walruses	**walruses'** teeth

A Use the possessive form of the noun in parentheses to complete each sentence. Write the sentence correctly.

1. My _____ boats are the *Hester* and the *Marie*. **(sons)**

   _____

2. Hester and Marie are my _____ names. **(daughters)**

   _____

3. The girls work on their _____ boat. **(cousins)**

   _____

4. The _____ job is to pull in the nets. **(girls)**

   _____

B 5–8. Use proofreading marks to correct the four plural possessive nouns in this part of a letter.

Example: The boys voices are loud.

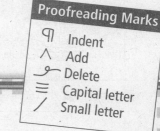

Proofreading Marks

¶ Indent
∧ Add
Delete
Capital letter
Small letter

Proofreading

-Seaside Hotel-

I hope you can visit us. My parents boat is at the seashore.

Many of our friends boats are there too. If you come, you will hear

my sisters laughter. You will hear the seagulls cries.

(continued)

Grade 3: Unit 2 Nouns *(Use with pupil book pages 76–77.)*
Skill: Students will form and will use plural possessive nouns.

WORKBOOK PLUS
TCAP PRACTICE

33

Name _____

9 Plural Possessive Nouns (continued from page 33)

Challenge

Look at this silly picture.
Read the sentence about it.

Example: The whales' pool is
very cool.

Now write a sentence about each silly picture below. Use a plural possessive noun in each sentence.

1. _____   4. _____

_____   _____

   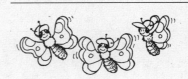

2. _____   5. _____

_____   _____

3. _____   6. _____

_____   _____

Writing Application: An Advertisement ——————

Suppose that you sell fish in a big market. People also sell fresh fruit, vegetables, and other foods at this market. Write five sentences that describe the market and the good things people can buy there. Use a plural possessive noun in each sentence.

© Houghton Mifflin Harcourt Publishing Company

Grade 3: Unit 2 Nouns *(Use with pupil book pages 76–77.)*
Skill: Students will form and will use plural possessive nouns.

Name _____

Using Exact Nouns

     robin   seeds

The ~~bird~~ ate the ~~food~~.

1–10. Change each underlined noun in this report to a more exact noun. Use one word from each pair of words in the Word Box. Cross out the weak noun and write the exact noun above it.

April	February	mud	soil
daisies	corn	sun	brightness
Joseph	Nina	wetness	rain
field	area	trees	cornstalks
tractor	truck	crates	holders

Revising

In spring, a farmer plants seeds. A girl works in the place. The
machine rolls over the ground. The seeds go into the ground. The plants
get plenty of light and liquid. Soon the plants are as tall as a person!
Many workers help pick the crops. Workers load the vegetables into
strong boxes. Soon, all the corn will be in the stores.

Grade 3: Unit 2 Nouns *(Use with pupil book page 78.)*
Skill: Students will replace weak nouns with more exact nouns.

WORKBOOK PLUS
TCAP PRACTICE

35

Name _____

1 What Are Verbs?

verb
The eagle **builds** a nest.
predicate
verb
The woman **watched** the eagles.
predicate

There is one verb in each sentence. Write the verb.

1. The eagle found twigs and branches. _____

2. It carried them to the top of a cliff. _____

3. It built its nest there. _____

4. It sat quietly in its nest. _____

5. Eagles catch small animals for food. _____

6. An eagle hunts for food every day. _____

7. The big bird flies high in the air. _____

8. Its sharp eyes see everything. _____

9. A small rabbit hops along. _____

10. The eagle spreads its huge wings. _____

11. It dives toward the rabbit. _____

12. The rabbit runs across the field. _____

13. It jumps quickly over a rock. _____

14. The rabbit hides safely in its hole. _____

15. The eagle returns to its nest. _____

16. It folds its strong wings. _____

17. The eagle closes its eyes. _____

18. It sleeps all through the night. _____

(continued)

Grade 3: Unit 3 Verbs *(Use with pupil book pages 98–99.)*
Skill: Students will identify verbs.

1 What Are Verbs? (continued from page 36)

Challenge

Harry invented the machine in the picture below. Try to figure out how the machine works.

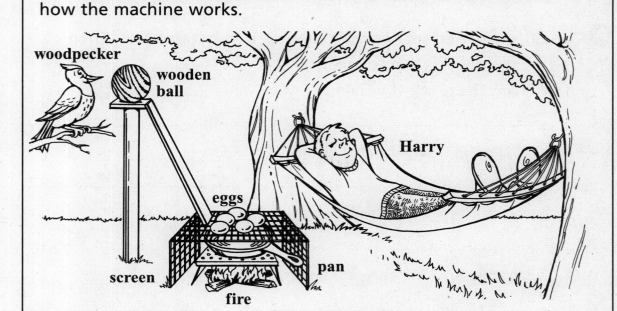

woodpecker

wooden ball

eggs

screen

fire

pan

Harry

Write a verb to complete each sentence about the machine.

1. The woodpecker _____ the ball.

2. The ball _____ down.

3. The ball _____ the eggs.

4. The eggs _____ into the pan.

5. The fire _____ the eggs.

6. Harry _____ the eggs.

Writing Application: A Report

DESCRIBING

Suppose you are a scientist. You have been studying the strange and unusual yura bird. Write a report about the yura bird. Describe at least five different things that the bird does. Circle each verb.

Grade 3: Unit 3 Verbs (Use with pupil book pages 98–99.)
Skill: Students will use verbs in sentences.

WORKBOOK PLUS
TCAP PRACTICE 37

2 Verbs in the Present

| Singular subject | One <u>captain</u> **steers** the ship. |
| Plural subject | Two <u>captains</u> **steer** their ships. |

A Underline the correct present time verb in parentheses. Then write each sentence correctly.

1. Workers (help, helps) us in many ways.

   _____

2. Mail carriers (bring, brings) our mail.

   _____

3. A doctor (keep, keeps) us healthy.

   _____

4. A librarian (choose, chooses) books.

   _____

B 5–10. Use proofreading marks to correct six present time verbs in this report.

Example: The workers in school ~~helps~~ us every day.
                                    help

Proofreading

Cities and towns needs many workers. Our

teacher tell us about the world. Bus drivers takes

us from place to place. Police officers keeps us safe. The

butcher sell us good meat to eat. All these workers makes

our lives better.

Proofreading Marks

¶	Indent
∧	Add
ꝑ	Delete
≡	Capital letter
/	Small letter

(continued)

Grade 3: Unit 3 Verbs *(Use with pupil book pages 100–101.)*
Skill: Students will choose present tense verbs to agree
with singular and plural subjects.

Name _____

2 Verbs in the Present (continued from page 38)

Challenge

Think of verbs that tell what the workers below are doing.

Describe what the workers are doing by completing the sentences below. Use a present time verb in each sentence.

1. Two workers _____.

2. One man _____.

3. Two women _____.

4. A worker _____.

Now draw two pictures of people working. Then write a sentence about each picture. Use a verb in the present time in each sentence.

<table>
<tr><td></td><td></td></tr>
</table>

5. _____

6. _____

Writing Application: A Letter

Suppose that you have a new job. Write a letter to a friend, describing your job and the people you work with. Use verbs in the present time. Underline the verbs.

Grade 3: Unit 3 Verbs *(Use with pupil book pages 100–101.)*
Skill: Students will use present tense verbs in sentences.

WORKBOOK PLUS
TCAP PRACTICE   39

3 More Verbs in the Present

Singular	Plural
One person **tosses** a ball.	Two people **toss** a ball.
One woman **washes** the car.	Two women **wash** the car.
One girl **catches** a bus.	Two girls **catch** a bus.
One man **fixes** the lamp.	Two men **fix** the lamps.
One boy **studies**.	Two boys **study**.

A Underline the correct present time verb in parentheses. Then write each sentence correctly.

1. Mike and I (rush, rushes) home from school.

_____

2. Mike (cross, crosses) the street carefully.

_____

3. A bus (splash, splashes) through puddles.

_____

B 4–8. Use proofreading marks to correct five present time verbs in this paragraph from a diary.

Example: Mom cry hello when we open the door.

Proofreading

Dear Diary,

Every afternoon my brother Mike dash

up the steps. He hurry into the house and

toss his backpack on a chair. Together we fixes peanut butter

and jelly sandwiches. Our dog, Zip, watch us.

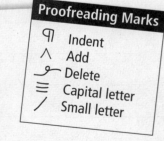

Proofreading Marks

¶ Indent
∧ Add
ℓ Delete
≡ Capital letter
/ Small letter

(continued)

40 **WORKBOOK PLUS**
TCAP PRACTICE

Grade 3: Unit 3 Verbs *(Use with pupil book pages 102–103.)*
Skill: Students will choose and will form present tense
verbs to agree with singular and plural subjects.

3 More Verbs in the Present (continued from page 40)

Challenge ⭐

Write a present time verb for each clue. Write one letter in each box or circle.

1. Opposite of *pulls* ⬭ ▢ ▢ ▢ ▢ ▢

2. Walks in a parade ▢ ⬭ ▢ ▢ ▢ ▢ ▢

3. Wipes the dishes ▢ ⬭ ▢ ▢ ▢ ▢

4. Repairs ▢ ⬭ ▢ ▢ ▢

5. Cleans her teeth ▢ ▢ ▢ ⬭ ▢ ▢ ▢

Now answer the riddle by writing the circled letters on the line below. Capitalize the first letter.

What is the capital city of France? _____

Writing Application: An Essay ———————

You are visiting the only factory in the world that makes yeckles. As you walk through the yeckle factory, you watch very carefully to see what is happening. Now write five sentences that tell how yeckles are made. Use a present time form of each verb from the Word Box.

mix	press	brush	stretch	dry

Grade 3: Unit 3 Verbs *(Use with pupil book pages 102–103.)*
  Skill: Students will write present tense verbs to agree with singular and plural subjects.

**WORKBOOK PLUS
TCAP PRACTICE**

41

Name _____

4 Verbs in the Past

Present	The children **watch** the experiment. The teachers **answer** questions.
Past	The children **watch<u>ed</u>** the experiment. The teachers **answer<u>ed</u>** questions.

A Write *present* if the underlined verb shows present time. Write *past* if the underlined verb shows past time.

1. Marta <u>pours</u> water into a pan. _____

2. Carlos <u>added</u> some salt. _____

3. Diane <u>mixed</u> the salt and water. _____

4. All the children <u>watch</u>. _____

5. The salt <u>disappeared</u> in the water. _____

6. The teacher <u>lights</u> the stove. _____

7. The teacher <u>heats</u> the water. _____

B Write the past time of the verb in parentheses to complete each sentence.

8. Soon the water _____ to steam. **(turn)**

9. The steam _____ away. **(drift)**

10. The children _____ into the pan. **(look)**

11. Some salt _____ on the bottom. **(stay)**

12. Boris _____ it on a scale. **(check)**

13. It _____ the same as before. **(weigh)**

14. The children _____. **(smile)**

15. They _____ questions about the experiment. **(ask)**

16. The teacher _____ them. **(answer)**

17. The children _____ about steam. **(learn)**

18. Everyone _____ the experiment. **(enjoy)**

(continued)

Grade 3: Unit 3 Verbs *(Use with pupil book pages 104–105.)*
Skill: Students will identify present and past tense verbs
and will form past tense verbs by adding *-ed*.

4 Verbs in the Past *(continued from page 42)*

Challenge

The children in the third grade class did a science experiment. Write six sentences, telling what the children did. Use a different past time verb in each sentence. The words in the picture may help you.

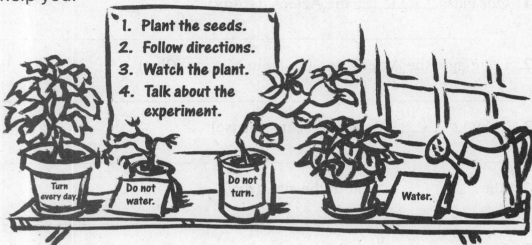

1. _____

2. _____

3. _____

4. _____

5. _____

6. _____

Writing Application: A Journal

Suppose that you are a scientist. You have made a great new discovery. Write about it in your journal. Use the past time form of each verb from the Word Box.

| discover | start | fill | want | learn |

Grade 3: Unit 3   Verbs   *(Use with pupil book pages 104–105.)*
Skill: Students will use regular past tense verbs correctly.

WORKBOOK PLUS
TCAP PRACTICE
43

Name _____

5 More Verbs in the Past

| share + -ed = shared | cry + -ed = cried | sip + -ed = sipped |

A Write each sentence using the correct past time form of the verb in parentheses.

1. Our class _____?_____ the Aztecs. **(study)**

_____

2. Long ago, the Aztecs _____?_____ in Mexico. **(live)**

_____

3. They _____?_____ corn and beans. **(raise)**

_____

4. They _____?_____ food in the sun. **(dry)**

_____

5. The Aztecs _____?_____ corn cakes over fires. **(bake)**

_____

B 6–10. Use proofreading marks to correct five past time verbs in this encyclopedia entry.

Example: On our trip to Mexico, I ~~slip~~ *slipped* when I climbed one of the pyramids.

Proofreading

Proofreading Marks	
¶	Indent
∧	Add
℘	Delete
≡	Capital letter
/	Small letter

Aztecs

The Aztecs rule a mighty empire. They live

about 500 years ago. They plan large cities. They

create beautiful pottery. Farmers plant corn, squash, and

other crops.

(continued)

Grade 3: Unit 3 Verbs *(Use with pupil book pages 106–107.)*
Skill: Students will form and will use the past tense of regular verbs that require spelling changes.

5 More Verbs in the Past (continued from page 44)

Challenge

The Aztecs had no alphabet. They used picture writing instead. Picture writing works something like this. Each picture stands for a word. Together they form sentences.

farmer	rabbit	basket	carry	drop	hop	spy
race	pat	past time	a the	into	away	

Figure out the meaning of each picture sentence below. Write each sentence. Remember that the picture ← after a verb means that the verb is in past time.

1. • ⚲ ( ) ← • ⊖ _____

2. • ⚘ ∞ ← ⌣ ⚲ _____

3. ⌣ ⚲ ↓ ← ⌣ ⊖ _____

4. ⌣ ⚘ ⌢ ← ⌣ ⌇ ⌣ ⊖ _____

5. ⌣ ⚘ --- ← = _____

Now write your own picture sentence. You can use the pictures above or make up some of your own. Put the pictures together to make a sentence. Then write the sentence in words.

6. [   ] _____

_____

Writing Application: A Magazine Article

You are digging in Mexico. You discover some old pots, tools, and baskets. Write an article, telling how people used these things long ago. Use the past time form of five verbs from the Word Box.

use	dip	carry	bake	scrub	dance	chop

Grade 3: Unit 3 Verbs *(Use with pupil book pages 106–107.)*
   Skill: Students will use the past tense of regular verbs that require spelling changes.

WORKBOOK PLUS TCAP PRACTICE 45

Name _____

6 Verbs in the Future

Present	Our class **visits** a museum every year.
Past	We **visited** a toy museum last year.
Future	This year we **will visit** a science museum.

A Use the future form of the verb in parentheses to complete each sentence.

1. Matt and Katy _____ a science museum tomorrow. **(visit)**

2. They _____ potato cells through a microscope. **(inspect)**

3. They _____ at the stars through a telescope. **(gaze)**

4. Matt and Katy _____ into outer space. **(peer)**

5. They _____ to the class on what they see. **(report)**

B 6–10. Read this trip plan. Use proofreading marks to correctly show five verbs in future time.

Example: Matt and Katy will ~~remembered~~ ^remember^ this trip for a long time.

Proofreading

We begin our visit to the museum in the insect

room. There we will explored the ant farms.

Next, we learn about dinosaurs. The space exhibit will showed

how astronauts live in space. We see the earliest spacecraft.

Proofreading Marks

¶	Indent
∧	Add
✄	Delete
≡	Capital letter
/	Small letter

(continued)

Grade 3: Unit 3   Verbs   *(Use with pupil book pages 108–109.)*
Skill: Students will use future tense verbs correctly.

6 Verbs in the Future (continued from page 46)

Challenge

You are about to visit a science museum. Draw pictures of four things you will see and do there. Then write a sentence about each picture. Use verbs in future time form.

1.	3.
2.	4.

1. _____

2. _____

3. _____

4. _____

Writing Application: A Space Story

You are an astronaut about to blast off for an exciting mission to a faraway planet. A newspaper reporter asks you what you think you will see. Write your answer in sentences using five future time verbs.

Grade 3: Unit 3 Verbs (*Use with pupil book pages 108–109.*)
Skill: Students will use future tense verbs correctly.

**WORKBOOK PLUS
TCAP PRACTICE**   **47**

Writing with Verbs

Two sentences	The eagle found twigs. The eagle built a nest.
Combined sentence	The eagle found twigs and built a nest.

Combining Sentences 1–5. Combine sentences that have the same subject by joining predicates. Put the word *and* between them.

Revising

The eagle hunts every day. The eagle catches small animals for food. It flies high in the air. It sees many things. A small, brown rabbit hops along the ground below. The eagle spreads its huge wings. The eagle dives toward the rabbit. The rabbit runs across the field, jumps over a rock, and escapes into the woods.

The eagle returns to its nest. The eagle folds its huge wings. The huge bird closes its eyes. The huge bird sleeps all night. Tomorrow it will spot another animal to hunt.

1. _____

_____

2. _____

_____

3. _____

_____

4. _____

_____

5. _____

_____

(continued)

Grade 3: Unit 3 Verbs *(Use with pupil book pages 110–111.)*
Skill: Students will combine sentences with the same subject.

Writing with Verbs (continued from page 48)

Two sentences	Marta pours water into a pan. Marta adds salt.
Combined sentences	Marta pours water into a pan and adds salt.
	Marta pours water into a pan, and Marta adds salt.

Combining Sentences 6–10. Combine sentences that have the same subject by joining predicates. Put the word *and* between them. You may leave in both subjects or take the second one out.

Revising

It is fun to cook when people work together. Sam's friends are making spaghetti and sauce for dinner. Diane watches the boiling water. Diane turns down the heat. When the water is boiling, Christine adds the spaghetti. Nicole opens the tomato sauce. Nicole measures the spices. Lee pours the sauce into the pan. Lee adds the meat. The sauce smells so good!

Chuck drains the spaghetti. Chuck puts it in a bowl. Mom calls everyone to come to the table. Dave dishes out the spaghetti. Dave pours the sauce. What a yummy meal!

6. _____

_____

7. _____

_____

8. _____

_____

9. _____

_____

10. _____

_____

Grade 3: Unit 3 Verbs *(Use with pupil book pages 110–111.)*
  Skill: Students will combine fluentces with the same subject.

WORKBOOK PLUS
TCAP PRACTICE

49

Name _____

7 The Special Verb *be*

| Present | I **am** in my yard. Rusty **is** my pet. We **are** outdoors. |
| Past | Dan **was** at school. Lottie **was** with him. They **were** busy. |

A Underline the correct verb in parentheses to complete each sentence.

1. I (am, are) curious about grasshoppers.

2. Grasshoppers (is, are) insects.

3. This grasshopper (am, is) green.

4. It (is, are) a good jumper.

5. Its hind legs (is, are) strong.

6. I (am, are) close to the grasshopper.

7. Walter (is, are) with me.

8. We (is, are) not afraid of the grasshopper.

B 9–14. Use proofreading marks to correct six verbs in this encyclopedia entry.

Example: That ant ~~were~~ was crawling down a hole into its nest.

Proofreading

INSECT

An insect are an animal with six legs. The

firefly am an insect. Butterflies is insects too!

Some insects is pests. The bee, on the other hand, are very

helpful. When we studied insects, the tiger beetle and the gypsy

moth was my favorites.

Proofreading Marks
¶ Indent
∧ Add
୧ Delete
= Capital letter
/ Small letter

(continued)

Grade 3: Unit 3 Verbs *(Use with pupil book pages 112–113.)*
Skill: Students will use present and past tense forms of the
verb *be* to agree with singular and plural subjects.

Name _____

7 The Special Verb *be* (continued from page 50)

Challenge

Look at the pictures below. Write sentences to tell what the insects say.

1. The big grasshopper says a sentence with the verb *am*.

_____

2. The small grasshopper says a sentence with the verb *are*.

_____

3. The butterfly says a sentence with the verb *is*.

_____

4. The ant says a sentence with the verb *were*.

_____

5. They all say a sentence with the verb *was*.

_____

Writing Application: An Interview

COMPARING AND CONTRASTING

Suppose that you are a grasshopper. A television reporter has come to ask you questions about your life now and your life as a baby grasshopper. Write the answers you will give. Use the verbs *am, is, are, was,* and *were.*

Grade 3: Unit 3 Verbs *(Use with pupil book pages 112–113.)*
Skill: Students will use present and past tense forms of the verb *be* with singular and plural subjects.

WORKBOOK PLUS
TCAP PRACTICE

51

8 Helping Verbs

Singular subjects	Water **has** turned to ice.
	She **has** learned about it.
Plural subjects	Waves **have** splashed me.
	We **have** watched the waves.

Write *has* or *have* to complete each sentence correctly.

1. We _____ learned much about the earth.

2. The earth _____ changed over many years.

3. Some islands _____ disappeared.

4. A new island _____ risen from the sea.

5. Whole forests _____ burned to the ground.

6. The rain _____ poured down.

7. It _____ washed soil away.

8. Streams _____ carried soil to new places.

9. The soil _____ become rich farmland.

10. Valleys _____ filled with water.

11. They _____ become new lakes.

12. This valley _____ become a river.

13. You _____ wondered what happens to mountains.

14. I _____ asked my teacher about this.

15. He _____ looked up the answer.

16. Some mountains _____ come from volcanoes.

17. Wind _____ worn down an old mountain.

18. This great mountain _____ turned into a hill.

19. Trees _____ grown on the hillside.

20. Birds _____ come to live here.

(continued)

Grade 3: Unit 3 Verbs *(Use with pupil book pages 114–115.)*
Skill: Students will use the helping verbs *has* and *have* correctly.

8 Helping Verbs (continued from page 52)

Challenge

Help the Waverly family row down the winding river. Draw a route through places where the helping verbs *has* and *have* are used correctly. Then cross out each incorrect helping verb and write the correct verb above it.

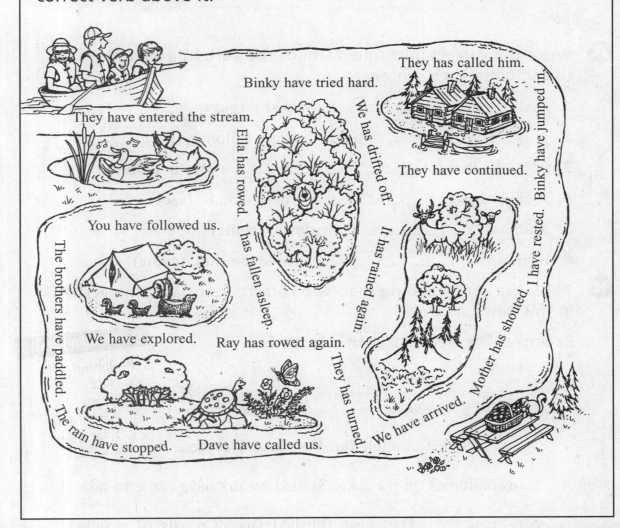

They has called him.

Binky have tried hard.

They have entered the stream.

We has drifted off.

They have continued.

It has rained again.

Ella has rowed. I has fallen asleep.

You have followed us.

The brothers have paddled.

We have explored.

Ray has rowed again.

They has turned.

Binky have jumped in. I have rested.

Mother has shouted.

We have arrived.

The rain have stopped.

Dave have called us.

NARRATING

Writing Application: A Story

Suppose that you are a very old mountain. You have been standing for many thousands of years. Write a story about your long life. Use the helping verb *has* or *have* in each sentence.

Grade 3: Unit 3 Verbs (*Use with pupil book pages 114–115.*)
Skill: Students will use the helping verbs *has* and *have* correctly.

WORKBOOK PLUS
TCAP PRACTICE

53

9 Irregular Verbs

Present	Past	With *has, have,* or *had*
go	**went**	(has, have, had) **gone**
see	**saw**	(has, have, had) **seen**
do	**did**	(has, have, had) **done**
run	**ran**	(has, have, had) **run**
come	**came**	(has, have, had) **come**

A Write the correct past time form of the verb in parentheses to complete each sentence.

1. A ship had _____ to sea. **(go)**

2. I _____ on the ship as a sailor. **(go)**

3. Polly the Parrot had _____ with me. **(come)**

4. A sailor has _____ dark clouds. **(see)**

5. Rain has _____ down. **(come)**

6. High waves _____ onto the ship. **(come)**

B 7–10. Use proofreading marks to correct four past time verbs in this news article.

Example: The captain had ~~ran~~ run onto the deck.

Proofreading Marks

¶	Indent
∧	Add
؍	Delete
≡	Capital letter
/	Small letter

We gone to watch the big race. We seen many sailboats on the lake. Skilled sailors have came to take part in a race. One boat finished first. Crowds of people cheered. Each crew has did its best.

(continued)

Grade 3: Unit 3 Verbs *(Use with pupil book pages 116–117.)*
Skill: Students will use the past and perfect tenses of irregular verbs.

9 Irregular Verbs (continued from page 54)

Challenge

Captain Sly gives Pedro Parrot a cracker each time he uses the right verb. Read the sentences that Pedro says. Write *cracker* beside the number for each sentence that has the right past time verb. Write the other sentences correctly.

1. The captain has saw a whale.

4. Waves have came onto the deck.

2. Many ships gone to the dock.

5. Captain Sly has done a good job.

3. The sailors ran to the rail.

6. The cook has ran to the kitchen.

1. _____

2. _____

3. _____

4. _____

5. _____

6. _____

How many crackers did Pedro Parrot get? _____

Writing Application: A Ship's Log

You are the captain of a ship. Each day you write in a big book called the ship's log. Write six sentences in the log about what has happened today. Use past time forms of the verbs *go*, *see*, *do*, *run*, and *come*.

Grade 3: Unit 3   Verbs   (Use with pupil book pages 116–117.)
Skill: Students will use the past and perfect tenses of irregular verbs.

WORKBOOK PLUS
TCAP PRACTICE

55

10 More Irregular Verbs

Present	Past	With *has*, *have*, or *had*
give	**gave**	(has, have, had) **given**
write	**wrote**	(has, have, had) **written**
eat	**ate**	(has, have, had) **eaten**
take	**took**	(has, have, had) **taken**
grow	**grew**	(has, have, had) **grown**

A Write the correct past time form of the verb in parentheses to complete each sentence.

1. Rice has _____ us many new dishes to eat. **(give)**

2. People in many lands have _____ rice. **(eat)**

3. Rice probably _____ first in Asia. **(grow)**

4. Most of the world's rice has _____ in China. **(grow)**

5. Chinese people _____ many kinds of rice dishes. **(eat)**

6. Sailors had _____ rice to other countries. **(take)**

7. Farmers have _____ it in warm, wet places. **(grow)**

8. Traders _____ rice for other goods. **(give)**

B 9–12. Use proofreading marks to correct four past time verbs in this report about traders.

Example: Traders ~~taken~~ ᵗᵒᵒᵏ many foods and brought them to new places around the world.

Proofreading Marks

¶	Indent
∧	Add
୨	Delete
=	Capital letter
/	Small letter

Proofreading

Long ago traders traveled the wide world. They take goods from one place to another. These traders have gave special foods to the world. People in many lands have ate these foods. Several authors have wrote about the adventures of traders.

(continued)

56 WORKBOOK PLUS
TCAP PRACTICE

Grade 3: Unit 3 Verbs *(Use with pupil book pages 118–119.)*
Skill: Students will use the past and perfect tenses of irregular verbs.

10 More Irregular Verbs (continued from page 56)

Challenge

Complete each sentence with the correct past time form of a verb from the Word Box. Then write the verbs in the puzzle.

| eat | take | write | grow |

ACROSS

1. Grandma has _____ a poem.

3. Meg had _____ the prize tomato.

4. Raccoons had _____ my lunch.

6. The twins have _____ an inch.

DOWN

1. Jen _____ her name on the list.

2. Our uncles have _____ us home.

3. Roses _____ here last year.

5. We _____ our umbrellas with us.

Writing Application: A Journal ——— DESCRIBING

Suppose that you are a trader long ago. You have traveled far and wide, buying and selling goods. Write at least six sentences in your journal. Describe the things you have traded, the places you have been, and the people you have met. Use the past time forms of the verbs *give, write, eat, take,* and *grow.*

Grade 3: Unit 3 Verbs *(Use with pupil book pages 118–119.)*
    Skill: Students will use the past and perfect tenses of irregular verbs.

**WORKBOOK PLUS
TCAP PRACTICE**   57

Name _____

11 Contractions with *not*

Two Words	Contraction
She **was not** going along.	She **wasn't** going along.
The girls **did not** wait.	The girls **didn't** wait.

A Write the contractions for the words in parentheses.

1. They _____ believe that the Tower of Pisa leaned. **(could not)**

2. They _____ seen anything else like it. **(have not)**

3. The tower _____ stand straight. **(does not)**

4. It _____ fallen over. **(has not)**

5. They _____ understand how it stays up. **(cannot)**

6. The builders _____ plan it that way. **(did not)**

7. There _____ any other towers like it. **(are not)**

B Write each sentence. Use two words in place of each contraction.

8. The tower isn't in the United States.

_____

9. Tanya and Dawn hadn't seen it before.

_____

10. They don't remember seeing pictures of it.

_____

11. Tanya wouldn't stand near the tower.

_____

12. They won't ever forget it!

_____

(continued)

Grade 3: Unit 3   Verbs   *(Use with pupil book pages 120–121.)*
Skill: Students will form contractions with *not*.

11 Contractions with *not* (continued from page 58)

Challenge

Write a contraction for each word or words. Write one letter or an apostrophe in each box or circle.

did not □ ○ □ □ □ □

will not □ □ □ □ ○

should not □ □ □ ○ □ □ □ □

were not □ □ □ ○ □ □ □

was not □ ○ □ □ □

cannot □ □ ○ □ □

has not □ □ ○ □ □

Now write the circled letters below to find the hidden sentence about a famous tower in Pisa, Italy. Begin the sentence with a capital letter.

_____

You are a builder. You tell workers how to build new buildings. The workers are making some mistakes on your newest building. Write six directions telling the builders what is wrong. Use a contraction with *not* in each direction.

Grade 3: Unit 3 Verbs *(Use with pupil book pages 120–121.)*
Skill: Students will form contractions with *not*.

WORKBOOK PLUS 59
TCAP PRACTICE

Name _____

Using Exact Verbs

            strolls   **saunters**

Ray ~~goes~~ down the path and ~~walks~~ across the bridge.

1–10. Change each underlined verb in this journal entry to a more exact verb. Use one word from each pair of words in the Word Box. Be sure the exact verb fits the meaning of the sentence. Cross out the weak verb and write the exact verb above it.

soars	bounces	waddles	splashes
drives	glides	chatters	cries
stroll	race	whispers	shouts
dashes	creeps	watch	study
stare	peek	ride	jump

Revising

Our jet plane <u>goes</u> across the country. The plane <u>comes</u> to

a stop on the runway. We all <u>get</u> off the plane in a hurry. Our

group <u>walks</u> quickly through the airport. In town, we <u>look</u> at

all the new things. We jump as a taxi <u>goes</u> through a puddle.

At the museum, our group <u>talks</u> about the paintings. The

guide <u>speaks</u> above all the noise. Then we <u>see</u> a beautiful

statue. Soon it's time to <u>take</u> the bus to our next stop.

Grade 3: Unit 3   Verbs   *(Use with pupil book page 122.)*
Skill: Students will replace weak verbs with more exact verbs.

1 What Are Adjectives?

| We like **quiet** music. | We heard a **large** band. |

A Write the adjective in each sentence.

1. Roberto and I went to a great concert. _____

2. People in the band wore black clothes. _____

3. The leader raised a short stick. _____

4. Beautiful music filled the room. _____

5. First, the band played a slow song. _____

6. They played a fast song after that. _____

7. A woman played a huge drum. _____

8. Loud sounds came from the drum. _____

B Write each adjective and the noun that it describes.

9. People played small drums too. _____

10. Others played shiny horns. _____

11. I liked the silver flutes. _____

12. They play high notes. _____

13. Roberto liked the large instruments. _____

14. They make deep sounds. _____

15. The band played a sad song at the end. _____

(continued)

Grade 3: Unit 4   Adjectives and Adverbs   *(Use with pupil book pages 142–143.)*
Skill: Students will identify adjectives and the nouns that they modify.

WORKBOOK PLUS
TCAP PRACTICE

61

Name _____

1 What Are Adjectives? *(continued from page 61)*

Challenge

Use adjectives to complete each song.

Do you see the _____ band?

Listen to their _____ beat.

Clap your hands, stamp your feet,

Up and down the _____ street.

I met a _____ queen,

Driving a _____ car.

She sang a _____ song,

And wore a _____ star.

Now write your own song on the lines below. Be sure to use an adjective in each line of your song.

_____

_____

_____

_____

_____

_____

Writing Application: A Review

DESCRIBING

Suppose that you write reviews for a newspaper. Write a review about a concert you have just heard. Use adjectives to describe the place, the music, and some of the instruments. Underline the adjectives.

Name _____

2 More Adjectives

Your body has **several** parts.

One part of your body pumps blood.

Your heart pumps blood through **many** tubes.

Write the adjective that tells *how many* in each sentence.

1. You have one heart in your body. _____

2. The heart pumps blood to many parts of the body. _____

3. It pumps five quarts of blood in a minute. _____

4. Two tubes go to the heart. _____

5. One tube brings blood into the heart. _____

6. Some blood is also carried away. _____

7. There are several doors inside the heart. _____

8. They let blood into the two sides of the heart. _____

9. Your heart beats about seventy times a minute. _____

10. Many hearts beat faster than this. _____

11. A few hearts beat more slowly. _____

12. An adult's heart is about five inches long. _____

13. It weighs about one pound. _____

14. Many animals have hearts too. _____

15. A few animals do not have hearts. _____

16. There are several ways to care for your heart. _____

17. One way is to eat well. _____

18. Getting some exercise helps your heart too. _____

(continued)

Grade 3: Unit 4   Adjectives and Adverbs   *(Use with pupil book pages 144–145.)*
Skill: Students will identify adjectives that tell how many.

**WORKBOOK PLUS
TCAP PRACTICE**   **63**

Name _____

2 More Adjectives *(continued from page 63)*

Challenge

This creature is a yellow spotted triff-eater. Write adjectives that tell *how many* to label the parts of the triff-eater's body.

_____ wings   _____ feelers

_____ tail   _____ eyes

_____ legs

                                                              _____ spots

_____ toes on each foot

Now write four sentences about one day in the life of a triff-eater. Use adjectives from the Word Box in your sentences.

many	several	few	some

1. _____

2. _____

3. _____

4. _____

Writing Application: A Story ————————————

NARRATING

Suppose that you are a tiny creature. You live inside a heart. Write a short story about what it is like inside this heart. Tell what you hear, see, and feel. Use five adjectives that tell *how many*.

64 WORKBOOK PLUS
TCAP PRACTICE

Grade 3: Unit 4 Adjectives and Adverbs *(Use with pupil book pages 144–145.)*
Skill: Students will use adjectives that tell how many.

Writing with Adjectives

| Without elaboration | The wind blew off my hat. |
| With elaboration | The <u>strong</u> wind blew off my hat. |

Elaborating Sentences 1–10. Elaborate the sentences in this journal entry by adding adjectives that describe each underlined noun. Rewrite the paragraph, making the changes.

Revising

We knew the storm was coming. The <u>clouds</u> gathered overhead. Our <u>teacher</u> told us to get our raincoats. We were going home early, before the <u>storm</u> hit. The <u>buses</u> waited for us outside. As we rode home, we could feel the <u>wind</u> getting stronger.

When I got home, everyone was busy. Dad had put up some <u>boards</u>. These would protect the <u>windows</u>. Mom and Jen had gathered some <u>flashlights</u>. Then we all went down into the <u>basement</u>. Everyone would be safe there until the <u>storm</u> was over.

_____

_____

_____

_____

_____

_____

_____

_____

_____

_____

(continued)

Grade 3: Unit 4   Adjectives and Adverbs   *(Use with pupil book pages 146–147.)*
Skill: Students will elaborate sentences by adding adjectives.

WORKBOOK PLUS
TCAP PRACTICE   65

Writing with Adjectives *(continued from page 65)*

Not combined	I have some yarn. It is fluffy.
Combined	I have some fluffy yarn.

Combining Sentences 11–15. Use the adjective to combine each underlined pair of sentences in this e-mail message. Then write the new sentences.

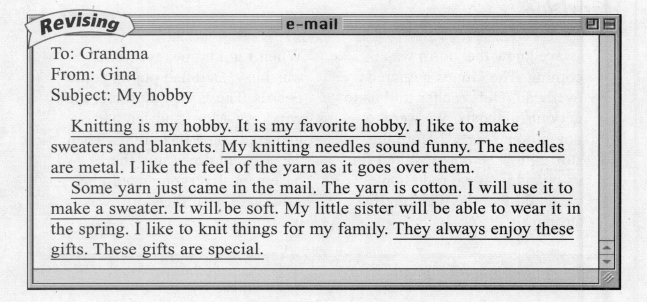

Revising ▢▢▢▢▢ **e-mail** ▢▢▢▢▢

To: Grandma
From: Gina
Subject: My hobby

   Knitting is my hobby. It is my favorite hobby. I like to make sweaters and blankets. My knitting needles sound funny. The needles are metal. I like the feel of the yarn as it goes over them.
   Some yarn just came in the mail. The yarn is cotton. I will use it to make a sweater. It will be soft. My little sister will be able to wear it in the spring. I like to knit things for my family. They always enjoy these gifts. These gifts are special.

11. _____

   _____

12. _____

   _____

13. _____

   _____

14. _____

   _____

15. _____

   _____

Grade 3: Unit 4 Adjectives and Adverbs *(Use with pupil book pages 146–147.)*
Skill: Students will combine sentences by moving adjectives.

3 Using *a, an,* and *the*

> One dinosaur had **a** l̲ong horn.
> That horn could scare away **an** e̲nemy.
> **The** end of the horn was sharp.
> **The** dinosaurs ruled the land.

A Write the correct article in parentheses to complete each sentence.

1. Mrs. Baker showed us _____ interesting picture. **(a, an)**

2. It showed _____ dinosaur. **(a, an)**

3. _____ dinosaurs were often very large. **(A, The)**

4. This dinosaur was much bigger than _____ elephant. **(a, an)**

5. It was much taller than _____ giraffe. **(a, an)**

6. _____ head was tiny. **(The, An)**

7. It had _____ flat beak. **(a, an)**

8. _____ smallest dinosaurs were the size of chickens. **(The, An)**

9. Dinosaurs lived _____ very long time ago. **(a, an)**

10. Some dinosaurs lived in _____ water. **(an, the)**

B 11–14. Use proofreading marks to write each article correctly in this news bulletin.

Example: We saw ~~an~~ ^a movie about dinosaurs today.

Proofreading Marks	
¶	Indent
∧	Add
ℐ	Delete
≡	Capital letter
/	Small letter

WARNING!

One dinosaur was spotted today on a

loose. His name is Rex. He is an tyrant. He is bigger than an

house. Can you imagine a animal that big?

(continued)

Grade 3: Unit 4   Adjectives and Adverbs   *(Use with pupil book pages 148–149.)*
Skill: Students will use articles correctly.

WORKBOOK PLUS
TCAP PRACTICE   **67**

3 Using *a*, *an*, and *the* (continued from page 67)

Challenge

Write a sentence to describe each dinosaur below. Use the article *a*, *an*, or *the* in each sentence.

1. _____
   _____
   _____

2. _____
   _____
   _____

3. _____
   _____
   _____

4. _____
   _____
   _____

Writing Application: A Play

Suppose that you are a famous writer. You are writing a short play about two dinosaurs who meet at a small pond. Name each dinosaur and decide why they are at the pond. Write what each dinosaur says. Use the articles *a*, *an*, and *the* in your play.

68   **WORKBOOK PLUS**
     TCAP PRACTICE

Grade 3: Unit 4   Adjectives and Adverbs   *(Use with pupil book pages 148–149.)*
Skill: Students will use articles correctly.

4 Comparing with Adjectives

Maine is an **old** state.
Ohio is an **older** state than Maine.
New York is the **oldest** state of the three.

A Choose the correct form of the adjective to complete each sentence. Write the sentence.

1. Rhode Island is the (smaller, smallest) of all the states.

_____

_____

2. Texas is a (smaller, smallest) state than Alaska.

_____

_____

3. Arkansas has (warmer, warmest) winters than Alaska.

_____

_____

4. Florida has the (warmer, warmest) winters of the three.

_____

_____

B 5–8. Use proofreading marks to correct the adjectives in this report.

deepest
Example: Which state has the ~~deeper~~ lake of all the states?
                                       ^

Texas is a larger state. It is largest than

Florida. But Alaska is the larger of all three. It is

also the colder of the three.

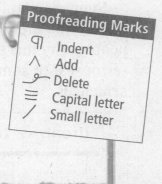

Proofreading Marks

¶ Indent
^ Add
ℐ Delete
≡ Capital letter
/ Small letter

(continued)

Grade 3: Unit 4   Adjectives and Adverbs   *(Use with pupil book pages 150–151.)*
Skill: Students will choose and will form comparative and superlative adjectives.

**WORKBOOK PLUS
TCAP PRACTICE**

69

4 Comparing with Adjectives (continued from page 69)

Challenge

The map below shows the states of Ecks, Wye, and Zee.

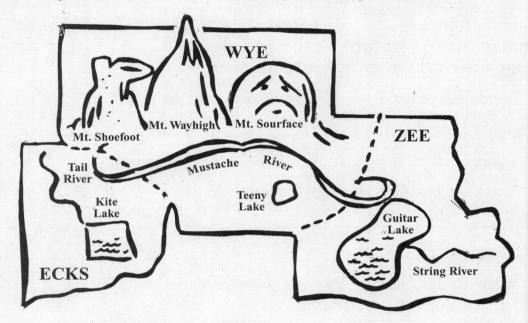

On another piece of paper, write six sentences, comparing the places on the map. Use forms of the adjectives from the Word Box in your sentences.

| high | tall | big | small | short | long |

Writing Application: A Guidebook

Suppose that the new state of Squeakland has been added to the United States. You are writing six sentences for Squeakland's guidebook. Tell people why this state is special and what places they should visit. Add -er or -est to some adjectives from the Word Box, and use them in your sentences.

| great | tall | new | old | warm | clean | fair |

70 WORKBOOK PLUS
TCAP PRACTICE

Grade 3: Unit 4   Adjectives and Adverbs   (Use with pupil book pages 150–151.)
Skill: Students will use comparative and superlative adjectives.

Name _____

5 What Are Adverbs?

Swiftly the snow falls.

It flies through the air **quietly**.

The children **quickly** put on their boots.

The sun shines **brightly** on the snow.

Write the adverb that tells *how* in each sentence.

1. Snow lies thickly on the ground. _____
2. The teacher speaks cheerfully. _____
3. The children move swiftly. _____
4. They dress warmly. _____
5. Firmly they fasten boots and jackets. _____
6. They hurry happily out the door. _____
7. They quietly stand in a circle. _____
8. Carefully they pick up some snow. _____
9. They look at it closely. _____
10. A special glass helps them see it clearly. _____
11. They plainly see six sides on each snowflake. _____
12. The children politely take turns with the glass. _____
13. Rosa patiently waits for her turn. _____
14. She holds some snow tightly. _____
15. Eagerly she looks through the glass. _____
16. Suddenly she sees that the snow is gone. _____
17. It melted quickly! _____
18. Her friends gladly bring her more. _____

(continued)

Grade 3: Unit 4   Adjectives and Adverbs   *(Use with pupil book pages 152–153.)*
Skill: Students will identify adverbs ending with -ly.   **WORKBOOK PLUS** 71
TCAP PRACTICE

Name _____

5 What Are Adverbs? *(continued from page 71)*

Challenge

Use adverbs that tell *how* to complete the crossword puzzle.

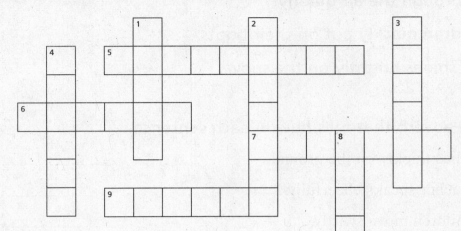

ACROSS

5. How you hold sharp things
6. How a lion roars
7. How you hold a kite string
9. How owls act in stories
10. How stars shine on cloudy nights

DOWN

1. How an unhappy person speaks
2. How you talk in a library
3. How your teacher wants you to write
4. How a turtle moves
8. How a truthful person speaks

Writing Application: A Journal ———————————— EXPRESSING

Suppose that you are a snowflake. You have had a very exciting day. Write five sentences in your journal, telling about this exciting day. Use an adverb that tells *how* in each sentence.

Grade 3: Unit 4 Adjectives and Adverbs *(Use with pupil book pages 152–153.)*
Skill: Students will use adverbs ending with *-ly*.

Name _____

6 Other Kinds of Adverbs

When	Nick **often** visits new places.
Where	His family travels **far**.

Underline the adverb in each sentence. Then write *when* or *where* for each adverb.

1. Yesterday Nick visited an old village. _____

2. Nick's family lived nearby. _____

3. Early settlers built the village here. _____

4. Many settlers traveled far. _____

5. Today visitors explore the village. _____

6. Nick saw old houses there. _____

7. Someone had planted small gardens everywhere. _____

8. Women brought out gardening tools and baskets. _____

9. They always wear long dresses. _____

10. Nick visited an old kitchen first. _____

11. Next, he looked at the sawmill. _____

12. Big logs were piled around. _____

13. Later, he watched a horse pull a plow. _____

14. Nick will return often. _____

(continued)

Grade 3: Unit 4 Adjectives and Adverbs *(Use with pupil book pages 154–155.)*
Skill: Students will identify adverbs that tell *when* and *where*.

WORKBOOK PLUS
TCAP PRACTICE

73

Name _____

6 Other Kinds of Adverbs (continued from page 73)

Challenge

You have found a message written by someone long ago. The adverbs in the message are scrambled to keep them secret. Unscramble them to figure out the message.

My ship left trayedeys. It will arrive moortrow. Go to the harbor and look dunora. Go dehaa when you see a sign for the Green Bird Inn. Wait for me aptrusis. I will come noso.

1. When did the ship leave?   _____

2. When will it arrive?   _____

3. Where should you look?   _____

4. Where should you go when you see the sign?   _____

5. Where should you wait?   _____

6. When will the person come?   _____

Now suppose that you are living in the future. Write a secret message to arrange a meeting on another planet. Use at least five adverbs that tell *when* or *where*. Be sure to scramble the letters in the adverbs.

_____

_____

_____

_____

Writing Application: A Report _____ DESCRIBING

Someone has invented a time machine. It can take you to the past or the future. Take a trip to another time. Write a report about the things you see and do. Use adverbs that tell *when* and *where*.

Grade 3: Unit 4 Adjectives and Adverbs *(Use with pupil book pages 154–155.)*
Skill: Students will use adverbs that tell *when* and *where*.

Name _____

Writing with Adverbs

| Without elaboration | Snow lies on the ground. |
| With elaboration | Snow lies <u>thickly</u> on the ground. |

Elaborating Sentences 1–10. Elaborate the sentences from this narrative by adding adverbs that describe each underlined verb. Rewrite the paragraph, making the changes.

Revising

It's time to <u>go</u> for recess. The teacher <u>speaks</u>. She tells the class to <u>put</u> on their coats. The children are excited about the snow. They <u>get dressed</u>. They fasten their boots and jackets. The children <u>pull</u> on their hats and mittens. When the teacher gives the signal, they <u>run</u>.

They <u>pick</u> up some snow. They pack the snow into shapes. Chris <u>presses</u> the snow. Then he builds a giant snowball. Everyone <u>helps</u>, and the class <u>has</u> a big snowman!

_____
_____
_____
_____
_____
_____
_____
_____
_____
_____

(continued)

Writing with Adverbs *(continued from page 75)*

| Not combined | We will make soup. We will make it soon. |
| Combined | We will make soup soon. |

Combining Sentences 11–15. Use the adverb to combine each underlined pair of sentences from this book about pioneers. Then write the new sentences.

Revising

It wasn't easy being a pioneer in the 1800s. The pioneers studied maps to find trails going west. They studied the maps carefully. They wanted the shortest, easiest route. They wanted it desperately. In areas without trails or roads, the pioneers used the rivers as their highways. For example, some pioneers floated down the Ohio River on flatboats. People could see trees. They could see them everywhere.

Did the pioneers understand the danger? Did they completely understand it? Wagons tipped over. They tipped over easily. Life was difficult on the westward trails.

11. _____

_____

12. _____

_____

13. _____

_____

14. _____

_____

15. _____

_____

Grade 3: Unit 4   Adjectives and Adverbs   *(Use with pupil book pages 156–157.)*
Skill: Students will combine sentences by moving adverbs.

7 Using *to*, *two*, and *too*

Words	Meanings	Examples
to	in the direction of	I go **to** the fair.
two	a number (2)	I went for **two** hours.
too	also, more than enough	My friend went **too**. Grandmother was **too** busy.

A Write *to*, *two*, or *too* to complete each sentence.

1. Grandmother took her paints _____ the harbor.

2. She took her brushes _____.

3. She painted for more than _____ hours.

4. Then it grew _____ dark for painting.

5. Grandmother carried everything back _____ the house.

6. She had painted _____ pictures of the harbor.

7. Grandmother and I took her paintings _____ the art fair.

8. Some paintings were _____ big for Grandmother's car.

9. She put a few paintings in her truck _____.

10. I like the _____ paintings of the harbor.

B **11–15.** Use proofreading marks to correct *to*, *two*, and *too* in this part of a letter.

Example: Other people like Grandma's paintings to.

(too inserted with caret above "to")

Proofreading

From the Desk of Grandma

Greetings from Grandmother's house! Today

we went too an art show. My friend Jana came

with us two. We only stayed to hours. We were

just to tired. But we will go too another show tomorrow.

Proofreading Marks

¶	Indent
∧	Add
⌐	Delete
≡	Capital letter
/	Small letter

(continued)

Grade 3: Unit 4 Adjectives and Adverbs *(Use with pupil book pages 158–159.)*
Skill: Students will use *to*, *two*, and *too* correctly.

WORKBOOK PLUS
TCAP PRACTICE

77

7 Using *to*, *two*, and *too* (continued from page 77)

Challenge ⭐

Look at the drawing. Then write sentences about this picture. Follow the directions given below.

1. Write a sentence about the lobsters. Use the word *to*.

_____

2. Write a sentence about the seagulls. Use the word *two*.

_____

3. Write a sentence about the whales. Use the word *too*.

_____

4. Write a sentence, naming the drawing. Use *to, two,* or *too*.

_____

Writing Application: An Art Review — EXPLAINING

You write articles for an art magazine. You have been to an art show and have seen many different paintings. Write an article, telling which paintings you liked and which you didn't like. Explain your reasons. Use the word *to, two,* or *too* in each sentence.

Grade 3: Unit 4 Adjectives and Adverbs *(Use with pupil book pages 158–159.)*
Skill: Students will use *to, two,* and *too* correctly.

Using Exact Adjectives

> scarlet
> Lisa wore a ~~colored~~ blouse and a ~~dark~~ skirt.
> black

1–10. Replace each underlined adjective in this journal entry with a more exact adjective from each pair of words in the Word Box. Be sure the exact adjective fits the meaning of the sentence. Cross out the weak adjective and write the exact adjective above it.

fantastic	interesting	mellow	fluffy
yummy	elegant	dark	harsh
moderate	gigantic	amber	violet
brilliant	smart	snowy	icy
hard	loud	crispy	soggy

Revising

Luis and I went to a <u>nice</u> concert. People in the orchestra wore <u>good</u> clothes. One man played a <u>large</u> drum. It was a <u>nice</u> silver color. The tuba made a <u>big</u> noise! The trumpets had a <u>soft</u> sound, not <u>hard</u> at all. The <u>brown</u> violins had a rich sound, like a waterfall. After the concert, we had some <u>cold</u> sodas and <u>hard</u> chips. It was a wonderful night!

Grade 3: Unit 4 Adjectives and Adverbs *(Use with pupil book page 160.)*
Skill: Students will replace weak adjectives with more exact adjectives.

WORKBOOK PLUS
TCAP PRACTICE

79

1 Correct Sentences

Statement	Our country has had many Presidents.
Question	Was Washington the first President?
Command	Tell me the name of our sixth President.
Exclamation	What a great President Lincoln was!

A Write each sentence correctly.

1. our class is holding a contest

_____

2. who can name all the Presidents

_____

3. make a list of all the names

_____

4. what a long list it is

_____

B 5–10. This paragraph has three missing capital letters and three missing or incorrect end marks. Use proofreading marks to correct each sentence.

Example: doesn't everyone know who our first President was**?**

our third President was Thomas Jefferson.

please tell me what you know about him did

you know he was a famous inventor How talented he was?

Proofreading Marks	
¶	Indent
∧	Add
✐	Delete
☰	Capital letter
/	Small letter

80 WORKBOOK PLUS
TCAP PRACTICE

Grade 3: Unit 5   Capitalization and Punctuation   *(Use with pupil book pages 178–179.)*
Skill: Students will capitalize and will punctuate sentences.

1 Correct Sentences *(continued from page 80)*

Challenge

Suppose that you are touring a museum that has pictures of the Presidents of the United States. Look at the pictures of the first three Presidents. Then follow the directions below the pictures.

George Washington   **John Adams**   **Thomas Jefferson**

1. Write a statement about George Washington.

_____

2. Write a question you would like to ask John Adams.

_____

3. Write a polite command you would like to give Thomas Jefferson.

_____

4. Write an exclamation about all three Presidents.

_____

Writing Application: A Letter

Write a letter to the President of the United States. Include statements, questions, polite commands, and exclamations in your letter. Begin each sentence with a capital letter and use correct end marks.

Grade 3: Unit 5   Capitalization and Punctuation   *(Use with pupil book pages 178–179.)*
   Skill: Students will capitalize and will punctuate sentences.

WORKBOOK PLUS TCAP PRACTICE   81

Writing Good Sentences

Statements	Robots are amazing. They can perform many tasks.
Other types of sentences	Robots are amazing! Can they perform many tasks?

Writing Different Types of Sentences 1–5. Change each underlined statement on this Web site to another type of sentence. The word in parentheses tells you the type of sentence to write.

Revising

There are some places that humans cannot yet explore by themselves. Robots can be sent to faraway planets. (question) You might want to think about what we could learn from them. (command) Robots can go to places where people cannot go. They can take pictures and gather samples. They send this data back to Earth. Robots can't tell us how it feels to discover something new, though. Robots can't do everything that humans do. (exclamation)

The use of robots does have other advantages. (question) They don't need air, food, or water. They can stand freezing cold and burning heat. Robots are really fantastic. (exclamation)

1. _____

_____

2. _____

_____

3. _____

_____

4. _____

_____

5. _____

(continued)

82   **WORKBOOK PLUS**
TCAP PRACTICE   **Grade 3:** Unit 5   Capitalization and Punctuation   *(Use with pupil book pages 180–181.)*
Skill: Students will write and will punctuate different kinds of sentences.

Name _____

Writing Good Sentences *(continued from page 82)*

Sentences	People need trees. Trees provide shade.
Combined sentence	People need trees **because** trees provide shade.

Combining Sentences 6–10. Combine the underlined sentences in this report, using the words in parentheses.

Trees are probably the best friends we have in nature. Trees are useful. They clean pollution from the air. (because) Trees give us fruits and nuts to eat. They give us syrup to put on waffles. They also give us wood for building. They have been cut down. (after) Our life would be much different without trees.

Trees need a lot of water. They can grow big and tall. (before) A large tree absorbs nearly 100 gallons of water each day! We study trees. We walk through the forest. (while) We see elm trees, oak trees, and willow trees. We are going to plant a tree. We finish our walk. (when)

6. _____

_____

7. _____

_____

8. _____

_____

9. _____

_____

10. _____

_____

Grade 3: Unit 5   Capitalization and Punctuation   *(Use with pupil book pages 180–181.)*   WORKBOOK PLUS   **83**
   Skill: Students will combine complete sentences, using *because, before, after,*
   when, or *while.*   TCAP PRACTICE

2 Capitalizing Proper Nouns

Every **September**, **Aunt Alba** visits **Mia L. Diaz** and us.
My aunt will take **Father** and me to a parade on **Saturday**.
She took her cat **Pirate** to the parade on **Labor Day**.

A Write each sentence correctly.

1. Our city had a big parade for columbus day.

   _____

2. That was in the month of october.

   _____

3. Our friends lila m. swan and sonny selha led the parade.

   _____

4. The parade was on friday instead of saturday this year.

   _____

5. I saw uncle dave and my aunt riding on a float.

   _____

6. My uncle was dressed like Christopher Columbus.

   _____

B 7–12. Use proofreading marks to write each proper noun correctly in this notice.

Example: My cousin paulette will lead the marching band.
                              ≡

Proofreading

This year the columbus day parade will be held

on October 12. Marchers will meet on the corner

of adams street. The grand marshal is mayor

rossetti. Please come and join the fun.

Proofreading Marks

¶	Indent
∧	Add
℘	Delete
≡	Capital letter
/	Small letter

© Houghton Mifflin Harcourt Publishing Company

(continued)

Grade 3: Unit 5 Capitalization and Punctuation *(Use with pupil book pages 182–183.)*
Skill: Students will identify and will capitalize proper nouns.

2 Capitalizing Proper Nouns (continued from page 84)

Challenge ⭐

Read the letter below. Draw three lines under each letter that should be capitalized.

22 Cook Street
Elmhurst, IL 60126
January 16, 2001

Dear Janice,

 Do you know olive p. norris? She gave a speech here one saturday last october or november. I went with ramona to hear her.

 Guess what uncle ed gave me! His cat pepper had five kittens. Now I have a new kitten named rosebud!

Your friend,

Leah

Write the letters that should be capitalized. _____

Now unscramble the letters to spell two words that complete the sentence below.

Always capitalize _____.

Writing Application: A Speech ────────────

 Suppose that you are the mayor of a city. Your city has a special holiday to honor an important person in the city's history. Write a speech about this person and the new holiday. Use a proper noun in each sentence of your speech.

Grade 3: Unit 5 Capitalization and Punctuation (Use with pupil book pages 182–183.)
 Skill: Students will identify and will capitalize proper nouns.

**WORKBOOK PLUS
TCAP PRACTICE** 85

3 Capitalizing Other Nouns

> Dela's grandparents live near **Lake Chapala** in **Mexico**.
> They flew over the **Gulf** of **Mexico** on their way to **Chicago**.

A Write each sentence correctly.

1. Dela's grandparents visited the united states of america.

   _____

2. Dela lives near lake michigan in the state of illinois.

   _____

3. Her family went to the city of chicago for two days.

   _____

4. Her grandmother liked the flowers in lincoln park.

   _____

B 5–12. Use proofreading marks to correct each proper noun on this post card.

Example: There are many statues on d̲earborn s̲treet.

Proofreading

I think chicago is a great place. It is

such an important city. Today we walked

along michigan avenue. Then we went to

the art institute of chicago. Tomorrow we will

visit the field museum. What a wonderful time

we are having!

Proofreading Marks

¶ Indent
∧ Add
⌐ Delete
☰ Capital letter
/ Small letter

(continued)

86 WORKBOOK PLUS
TCAP PRACTICE

Grade 3: Unit 5   Capitalization and Punctuation   *(Use with pupil book pages 184–185.)*
Skill: Students will identify and will capitalize proper nouns.

3 Capitalizing Other Nouns (continued from page 86)

Challenge

You just moved to a town named Turtle Town. Turtle Town is unusual because each place is named for an animal. Write a name for each place shown on the map of Turtle Town below.

TURTLE TOWN

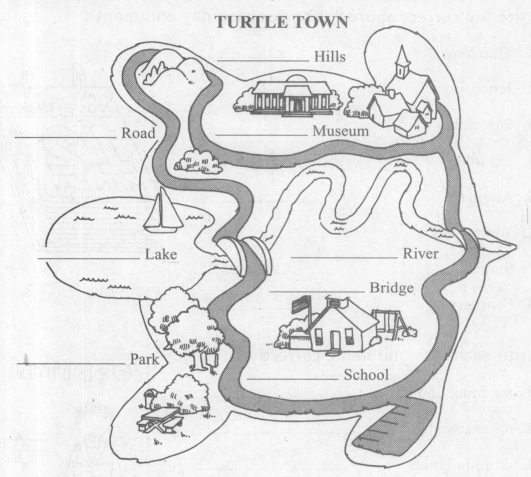

_____ Hills

_____ Road

_____ Museum

_____ Lake

_____ River

_____ Bridge

_____ Park

_____ School

On another piece of paper, write six sentences about a drive in Turtle Town. Use a different proper noun in each sentence.

Writing Application: A Travel Guide

DESCRIBING

You are writing a travel guide for your own city or town. Tell visitors about interesting places such as lakes, parks, rivers, and schools. Underline the proper nouns.

Grade 3: Unit 5 Capitalization and Punctuation (Use with pupil book pages 184–185.)
Skill: Students will use proper nouns in sentences.

WORKBOOK PLUS
TCAP PRACTICE
87

Name _____

4 Abbreviations

Days	Tuesday	**Tues.**	Friday	**Fri.**
Months	March	**Mar.**	October	**Oct.**
Titles	Mister	**Mr.**	Doctor	**Dr.**

A Write the correct abbreviation for each day and month.

1. Thursday _____

2. January _____

3. September _____

4. Saturday _____

5. August _____

6. Wednesday _____

7. Sunday _____

8. February _____

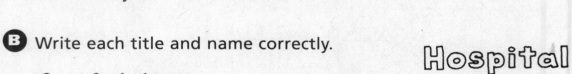

B Write each title and name correctly.

9. mr frank chong _____

10. ms marisa alves _____

11. dr anita lynch _____

12. miss flo rivers _____

13. mrs sara varga _____

14. dr. bert king _____

(continued)

Grade 3: Unit 5   Capitalization and Punctuation   *(Use with pupil book pages 186–187.)*
Skill: Students will write abbreviations correctly.

Name _____

4 Abbreviations (continued from page 88)

Challenge

You are a travel agent. You help customers plan their vacations. Read these notes about your customers' travel plans. Draw three lines under each letter that should be capitalized. Add periods where they are needed.

1. dr carol lamb	2. mr mateo sanchez
leaves wednesday, january 1	leaves saturday, march 22
returns saturday, february 1	returns sunday, may 4

Now use the names and dates from the notes to fill in the travel schedule below. Use abbreviations for each title, day, and month.

	LEAVES		RETURNS	
Person	Day	Month/date	Day	Month/date
1.				
2.				

On another piece of paper, make a list of six special events for your class or a club that you belong to. Write the day and the month for each event. Use correct abbreviations.

Writing Application: A Journal

Suppose that you are traveling around the world. You travel by boat, by train, by bus, and on foot. Write a journal, telling about six days of your trip. Include each day's date and the names and titles of the people you meet along the way. Use abbreviations correctly.

Grade 3: Unit 5 Capitalization and Punctuation (Use with pupil book pages 186–187.)
Skill: Students will write abbreviations correctly.

WORKBOOK PLUS
TCAP PRACTICE
89

© Houghton Mifflin Harcourt Publishing Company

Name _____

5 Book Titles

Did Gipp like the book **A Hot, Thirsty Day**?
Carla read poems from the book **The House in the Woods**.

Write each book title correctly.

1. sumi's prize _____

2. the birthday visitor _____

3. herman the helper _____

4. the star in the pail _____

5. a special trade _____

6. angus and the ducks _____

7. sunday for sonya _____

8. midnight on the mountain _____

Challenge

Look at the book covers below. Make up a title for each book, and write it below its cover. Use underlining and capital letters correctly.

_____   _____

_____   _____

On another piece of paper, draw your own book cover. Write the title of the book on the cover.

Grade 3: Unit 5   Capitalization and Punctuation   (Use with pupil book page 188.)
Skill: Students will write book titles correctly.

6 Introductory Words

> First, we got two bottles and some ice. Then we started our experiment. No, we didn't know what would happen.

Place commas where they are needed in these sentences.

1. Yes our class did a science experiment.

2. First we filled a bottle with very hot water.

3. Second we filled another bottle with cold water.

4. Next we poured most of the water out of both bottles.

5. Then we held some ice on the top of each bottle.

6. Well a cloud formed in one bottle.

7. Yes it was the bottle with the hot water in it.

8. No there was no cloud in the other bottle.

9. Then we talked about the experiment.

10. Finally we understood why the cloud had formed.

Challenge

Look at the pictures below. Write a sentence about each picture to describe the experiment. Use *yes, no, well,* or an order word at the beginning of each sentence.

1. _____

2. _____

3. _____

Grade 3: Unit 5   Capitalization and Punctuation   *(Use with pupil book page 189.)*
Skill: Students will use commas after introductory words.

**WORKBOOK PLUS
TCAP PRACTICE**   **91**

7 Commas in a Series

Nancy, Felipe, and Dale learn about America.
They read, write, and draw in class.

A Write each sentence correctly. Add commas where they are needed.

1. Canada Mexico and Peru are American countries.

   _____

2. Canada has mines for gold coal and iron.

   _____

3. People hike fish and camp in Canada's mountains.

   _____

4. Farmers in Canada grow wheat oats and potatoes.

   _____

5. Paper wood and oil come from Canada too.

   _____

6. Mexico has deserts mountains and jungles.

   _____

B 7–12. Add six commas to correct the sentences in this report about Mexico.

Example: Mexico has many gifted artists,musicians,and dancers.

A high plateau is in the center of Mexico. Around it are mountains on the east west and south. Mexico produces oil iron and silver. Its farmers grow sugar fruit and corn.

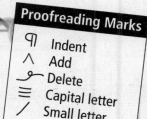

Proofreading Marks

¶ Indent
∧ Add
⌐ Delete
≡ Capital letter
/ Small letter

(continued)

92 **WORKBOOK PLUS**
TCAP PRACTICE

Grade 3: Unit 5 Capitalization and Punctuation *(Use with pupil book pages 190–191.)*
Skill: Students will use commas in a series.

Name _____

7 Commas in a Series (continued from page 92)

Challenge

Write six sentences about the picture below. In each sentence, use a series of three or more words.

1. _____

2. _____

3. _____

4. _____

5. _____

6. _____

Writing Application: A Magazine Article

DESCRIBING

    You write articles for a magazine. Write five sentences for an article about the imaginary country of Thumpia. Describe the crops, jobs, and weather in Thumpia. Use a series of three or more words in each sentence.

Grade 3: Unit 5 Capitalization and Punctuation *(Use with pupil book pages 190–191.)*
   Skill: Students will use commas in a series.

Writing Good Sentences

Short, choppy sentences	Thomas Edison invented the phonograph. Thomas Edison invented the telephone. Thomas Edison invented the projector.
Combined sentence	Thomas Edison invented the phonograph, the telephone, and the projector.

Combining Sentences to Make a Series 1–5. Combine each underlined group of sentences in this report. Write the new sentences below.

Revising

Inventors have created some wonderful things. One important invention is the car. The car changed how people live. The car changed how people work. The car changed how people travel. Our country was different after cars were invented. Drivers needed roads. Drivers needed bridges. Drivers needed fuel. Cars can cause problems, though. Cars can be noisy. Cars can be dirty. Cars can be annoying.

Other inventions help people have fun. Many families have radios. Many families have TVs. Many families have VCRs.

Some inventions make our work easier. Computers are useful to people. Microwaves are useful to people. Dishwashers are useful to people. Which invention do you use the most?

1. _____

_____

2. _____

_____

3. _____

_____

4. _____

_____

5. _____

_____

(continued)

Grade 3: Unit 5 Capitalization and Punctuation *(Use with pupil book pages 192–193.)*
Skill: Students will combine sentences by putting words in a series.

Name _____

Writing Good Sentences *(continued from page 94)*

Choppy sentences	Lasers erase old scars. Lasers measure distances. Lasers predict earthquakes.
Combined sentences	Lasers erase old scars, measure distances, and predict earthquakes.

Combining Sentences to Make a Series 6–10. Combine sentences in this book about technology by putting the groups of words in a series.

Revising

Lasers are sharper than a razor. Lasers are hotter than fire. Lasers are brighter than the sun. Lasers are amazing! They can read price codes. They can track airplanes. They can carry information. Eye doctors use lasers. Toolmakers use lasers. Diamond cutters use lasers.

Lasers are not only for work! People use lasers to create light shows. People use lasers to make photographs. People use lasers to record music. CD players make use of lasers. The first CDs were sold in 1982. Today they have replaced records for several reasons. CDs last longer than records. CDs hold more music. CDs take up less space.

The laser is truly an invention with many surprising uses.

6. _____

7. _____

8. _____

9. _____

10. _____

Grade 3: Unit 5 Capitalization and Punctuation *(Use with pupil book pages 192–193.)*
Skill: Students will combine sentences by putting groups of words in a series.

WORKBOOK PLUS
TCAP PRACTICE

95

8 Quotation Marks

> Bruno asked, "Why did people make arrowheads?"
> Jill replied, "They used them for hunting."

Write each sentence correctly. Add quotation marks where they are needed.

1. Jill said, Look at this old arrowhead.

_____

2. Jill added, It was made by people long ago.

_____

3. Bruno asked, What is it made of?

_____

4. Jill answered, This one is made of a stone called flint.

_____

5. Jill said, Arrowheads are made from other stones too.

_____

6. Bruno exclaimed, You know so much about arrowheads!

_____

7. Bruno asked, How did you learn about them?

_____

8. Jill answered, I read books about them.

_____

9. Jill added, I have seen arrowheads in museums too.

_____

10. Bruno said, I want to learn more about arrowheads.

_____

(continued)

96 WORKBOOK PLUS
TCAP PRACTICE

Grade 3: Unit 5 Capitalization and Punctuation *(Use with pupil book pages 194–195.)*
Skill: Students will use quotation marks in direct quotations.

Name _____

8 Quotation Marks (continued from page 96)

Challenge

Each arrowhead has a scrambled word on it. Together these words will form a mystery sentence. First, unscramble each word.

 yaSmm

 tramS

 idas

1. _____   2. _____   3. _____

 hrworsAaed

4. _____

 rea

 yerv

 dlo

5. _____   6. _____   7. _____

Now complete the mystery sentence by writing the unscrambled words in the numbered spaces below. Add quotation marks to show the speaker's exact words.

1. _____   2. _____   3. _____,

4. _____   5. _____   6. _____   7. _____.

Writing Application: An Interview _____ EXPLAINING

You are a scientist. You have dug up many arrowheads, tools, and pots from long ago. A television reporter has come to ask questions about your discoveries. Write six sentences that you and the reporter might say to each other. Use quotation marks to show each person's exact words.

© Houghton Mifflin Harcourt Publishing Company

Grade 3: Unit 5   Capitalization and Punctuation   *(Use with pupil book pages 194–195.)*
   Skill: Students will write direct quotations correctly.

**WORKBOOK PLUS
TCAP PRACTICE**   97

Name _____

9 More About Quotation Marks

Dion said, "My pencil is six inches long."
Kari asked, "Did you measure it with this ruler?"

A Write these sentences correctly. Add commas, capital letters, end marks, and quotation marks where they are needed.

1. Dion asked How many inches are in a foot?

   _____

2. Kari answered, "there are twelve inches in a foot"

   _____

3. Luis added "there are three feet in a yard."

   _____

4. Kari asked "is a yard longer than a meter"

   _____

5. Dion replied, A meter is a little longer than a yard

   _____

B 6–12. Use proofreading marks to add correct punctuation and capitalization to the sentences in these directions.

Example: Kari said‸, "Thanks for the help, Dion. You help lots of people."

Proofreading

Do you know the way to the post office " asked

the driver.

"it is only three blocks away" answered Dion.

"Just drive to the corner and turn left

"Thank you very much," said the driver. I think I can find it now."

Proofreading Marks	
¶	Indent
∧	Add
⌿	Delete
≡	Capital letter
/	Small letter

(continued)

© Houghton Mifflin Harcourt Publishing Company

Grade 3: Unit 5   Capitalization and Punctuation *(Use with pupil book pages 196–197.)*
Skill: Students will capitalize and will punctuate direct quotations.

Name _____

9 More About Quotation Marks (continued from page 98)

Challenge

Look at the picture below of Kate, Sherman, and Binh at their first club meeting. They are trying to decide which animal would make the best club pet.

What do you think Kate, Sherman, and Binh are saying about their pets? Write a quotation to complete each sentence below.

Kate asked _____

Sherman answered _____

Binh exclaimed _____

Sherman said _____

Kate added _____

Binh asked _____

Sherman replied _____

Kate exclaimed _____

Writing Application: A Conversation   EXPRESSING

You and two friends are building a secret clubhouse. You have to measure, cut, and nail together some boards for the clubhouse walls. Write six sentences to show what you and your friends might say as you work. Use a quotation in each sentence.

Grade 3: Unit 5   Capitalization and Punctuation   *(Use with pupil book pages 196–197.)*
Skill: Students will write direct quotations correctly.

WORKBOOK PLUS
TCAP PRACTICE   99

1 Subject Pronouns

Nouns	Subject Pronouns
Charles paints pictures.	He paints pictures.
The pictures are bright.	They are bright.

Write each sentence. Replace the underlined word or words with a subject pronoun. Be sure to underline titles of paintings just as you would underline titles of books.

1. Charles and I went to a museum in the city.

   _____

2. The museum had many paintings by Mary Cassatt.

   _____

3. Mary Cassatt was a famous American painter.

   _____

4. Did Cassatt live in France?

   _____

5. France has been the home of many artists over the years.

   _____

6. Painters have worked and shared ideas there.

   _____

7. Charles loves one of Cassatt's paintings called *The Bath*.

   _____

8. This painting is truly beautiful.

   _____

9. The museum was our favorite place.

   _____

10. Charles and I spent all afternoon in one room.

   _____

(continued)

© Houghton Mifflin Harcourt Publishing Company

100 WORKBOOK PLUS
TCAP PRACTICE

Grade 3: Unit 6 Pronouns *(Use with pupil book pages 214–215.)*
Skill: Students will use subject pronouns to replace nouns.

Name _____

1 Subject Pronouns (continued from page 100)

Challenge

Charles painted a large picture showing what he thought things would look like in the future. Each small picture below is a part of his big painting. Write a sentence that describes each picture. Begin each sentence with a subject pronoun.

1.  _____
   _____
   _____

2.  _____
   _____
   _____

3.  _____
   _____
   _____

4. 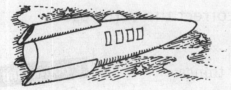 _____
   _____
   _____

On another piece of paper, draw your idea of a scene from the future. Write a description of your picture. Use subject pronouns in your sentences.

Writing Application: A Description

DESCRIBING

   Suppose that you and three friends are doing an art project in school. Write a short description of your project. Use at least five subject pronouns.

Grade 3: Unit 6   Pronouns   (Use with pupil book pages 214–215.)
Skill: Students will use singular and plural subject pronouns.

WORKBOOK PLUS
TCAP PRACTICE

101

Name _____

2 Pronouns and Verbs

> She **takes** some special paper.   I **take** some special paper.
> It **matches** Mr. Ito's paper.   They **match** Mr. Ito's paper.
> He **makes** a bird.   We **make** a bird.

A Write the correct verb form in parentheses to complete each sentence.

1. We _____ paper folding from Mr. Ito. **(learn, learns)**

2. He _____ from the country of Japan. **(come, comes)**

3. He _____ the art of paper folding to us. **(teach, teaches)**

4. I _____ a bird with Lynda. **(make, makes)**

5. She _____ the paper carefully. **(fold, folds)**

6. I _____ the paper flat. **(press, presses)**

7. She _____ up the folded paper. **(open, opens)**

8. You _____ the bird's neck now. **(see, sees)**

9. It _____ out so far! **(stretch, stretches)**

10. She _____ the wings next. **(make, makes)**

B 11–16. Use proofreading marks to correct the verbs used incorrectly in this diary entry.

Example: We ~~likes~~ making these pretty things.

 Proofreading

Proofreading Marks

¶	Indent
∧	Add
ℒ	Delete
≡	Capital letter
/	Small letter

Dear Diary,

In class we watches Mr. Ito. He make paper swans.

They looks so beautiful. One has big wings. It seem ready to fly.

We wants to learn more about paper folding. I thinks it is a

wonderful art.

(continued)

Grade 3: Unit 6 Pronouns *(Use with pupil book pages 216–217.)*
Skill: Students will choose correct verb forms to agree with pronoun subjects.

2 Pronouns and Verbs (continued from page 102)

Challenge

Lynda made a puzzle from a paper circle. Find a verb from the Word Box to go with each subject pronoun in the outer circle. Write these verbs in the correct spaces of the inner circle.

trade
wishes
fixes
stop
climb
hides
cries
sit
jump

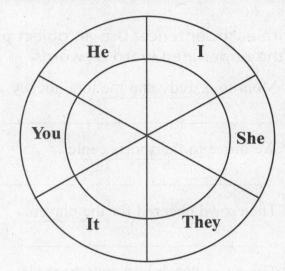

Now write sentences that begin with the pronouns and verbs that you matched in the puzzle. Add words to complete each sentence.

1. _____

2. _____

3. _____

4. _____

5. _____

6. _____

Writing Application: A Story

Suppose that a paper bird meets two real birds. Write a short story to describe what happens. Use a subject pronoun and a present time verb in each sentence.

Grade 3: Unit 6 Pronouns (Use with pupil book pages 216–217.)
Skill: Students will choose correct verb forms to agree with pronoun subjects.

WORKBOOK PLUS
TCAP PRACTICE

103

© Houghton Mifflin Harcourt Publishing Company

3 Object Pronouns

Nouns	Object Pronouns
I invited <u>Judy</u>.	I invited **her**.
Judy sat on <u>a bench</u>.	Judy sat on **it**.
Judy went with <u>Mom and Bart</u>.	Judy went with **them**.

A Write each sentence. Use an object pronoun to take the place of the underlined word or words.

1. Mom took <u>Judy and me</u> to a hockey game.

_____

2. We drove to <u>the sports center</u>.

_____

3. The crowd cheered for <u>the players</u>.

_____

4. The noise didn't bother <u>Judy</u> at all.

_____

5. The goalie never let <u>the puck</u> into the net.

_____

B Write the correct pronoun in parentheses to complete each sentence.

6. One time, the puck flew right at _____. **(us, we)**

7. That scared _____ for a minute. **(me, I)**

8. Then the goalie waved at _____. **(we, us)**

9. Judy waved back to _____. **(he, him)**

10. We took _____ home after the game. **(her, she)**

11. Judy thanked _____ many times. **(us, we)**

12. She wants to come with _____ again. **(I, me)**

(continued)

© Houghton Mifflin Harcourt Publishing Company

Grade 3: Unit 6 Pronouns *(Use with pupil book pages 218–219.)*
Skill: Students will use object pronouns to replace nouns.

Name _____

3 Object Pronouns (continued from page 104)

Challenge

Read these sentences about a hockey game. Put a check beside each sentence that has an object pronoun.

1. The c<u>o</u>ach watches us closely. _____

2. This big game is <u>i</u>mportant to her. _____

3. The <u>o</u>ther team beat us last night. _____

4. They shot the puck ac<u>r</u>oss the ice. _____

5. The p<u>u</u>ck zipped toward me suddenly! _____

6. The g<u>o</u>alie was ready for it. _____

7. Someo<u>n</u>e shot the puck at him quickly. _____

8. He block<u>e</u>d the play beautifully. _____

9. Noisy f<u>a</u>ns cheered for us! _____

10. We shouted with the<u>m</u>. _____

Look at the sentences that have check marks. Write the underlined letters from these sentences on the hockey players' uniforms below. Write only one letter on each uniform.

Now unscramble the letters on the uniforms to find the secret word.

Secret Word: _____

Writing Application: A Report

You are a TV sports announcer. Choose a real or an imaginary sport. Write a report that tells your TV audience about the game you are watching. Use an object pronoun in each sentence.

Grade 3: Unit 6 Pronouns *(Use with pupil book pages 218–219.)*
Skill: Students will use singular and plural object pronouns.

WORKBOOK PLUS
TCAP PRACTICE   105

Writing with Pronouns

Too many pronouns	Mr. Kwan goes bowling. He does it well. He likes it most of all. It is Mr. Kwan's favorite sport.
Better use of pronouns	Mr. Kwan goes bowling. He does it well. He likes bowling most of all. Bowling is Mr. Kwan's favorite sport.

Writing Clearly with Pronouns 1–5. Rewrite each underlined sentence in this story. Replace one pronoun in each sentence with a noun.

Revising

Mr. Kwan and his family go bowling at least once a week. He always goes with them on Friday nights. Mrs. Kwan and her daughter, Julie, belong to the same league. She also bowls in a Girl Scout league with her friends. She is the best one in it.

Julie and her brother take lessons with a pro. They take them with him on Sunday afternoons. They make Julie and her brother better bowlers. That makes bowling even more fun!

1. _____

_____

2. _____

_____

3. _____

_____

4. _____

_____

5. _____

_____

(continued)

Grade 3: Unit 6 Pronouns *(Use with pupil book pages 220–221.)*
Skill: Students will identify repetitive pronouns and change them to nouns for clarity.

Writing with Pronouns (continued from page 106)

| Not combined | Lacrosse is a difficult sport. Lacrosse takes a lot of strength. |
| Combined | Lacrosse is a difficult sport, and it takes a lot of strength. |

Combining Sentences 6–10. Combine the underlined sentences in this report by changing a noun to a pronoun.

Revising

Different sports use one kind of muscle more than another. Hockey players need to have very strong legs. Hockey players also depend on strong arms. Swimmers work on their shoulders. Swimmers make sure that their upper legs are in good shape. This helps them move swiftly through the water without getting tired. A tennis player also works on her upper legs. A tennis player needs to have strong arms as well. Bobsledders build strength in their stomachs. Bobsledders need good back muscles too. They use their stomach and back muscles to help control the bobsled. A gymnast usually works on all his muscles. A gymnast concentrates on certain muscles for special skills. For example, a gymnast working on the rings might build up his arms more than someone who works on the balance beam.

6. _____

_____

7. _____

_____

8. _____

_____

9. _____

_____

10. _____

_____

Name _____

4 Using *I* and *me*

| I drink milk every day.
Milk is good for **me**. | <u>Ying and I</u> are friends.
Ying visits <u>Tom and **me**</u>. |

A Choose the correct word or words in parentheses to complete each sentence. Write the sentence.

1. Ying showed (me and Tom, Tom and me) a milk carton.

_____

2. (I, Me) saw the word *pasteurized* on the carton.

_____

3. (Tom and me, Tom and I) wondered why.

_____

4. Ying gave a book to (me and Tom, Tom and me).

_____

5. (Tom and I, Tom and me) read about Louis Pasteur.

_____

B 6–10. Use proofreading marks to write *I* and *me* correctly in this book report.

Tom and I
Example: ~~Me and Tom~~ learned a lot.

Proofreading Marks
¶ Indent
∧ Add
⌐ Delete
≡ Capital letter
/ Small letter

Proofreading

Thanks to Louis Pasteur, milk is now safe

for you and I. This book taught Tom and I that

germs can grow in milk. Tom and me learned that Pasteur

heated milk to kill germs. Louis Pasteur's work helped you and I.

My classmates and me understand this now.

(continued)

Grade 3: Unit 6   Pronouns   *(Use with pupil book pages 223–223.)*
Skill: Students will use *I* and *me* correctly.

4 Using *I* and *me* (continued from page 108)

Challenge

Look at the picture below. Pete is teaching Eva and Mel how to make butter by hand.

Now read Mel's report about making butter. Mel has written the sentences in the wrong order. He has also made mistakes using the pronouns *I* and *me*. Write Mel's sentences correctly. Be sure to put them in the right order.

> Me and Eva found that the cream had turned to butter.
> Pete told Eva and I to pour the cream into the churn.
> Pete and me took the butter out of the churn.
> Pete wanted me and Eva to take turns beating the cream.

1. _____

2. _____

3. _____

4. _____

Writing Application: A Report

EXPLAINING

You are a scientist. You and your partner, Olga, have discovered a new way to keep food from spoiling. Write a short report that describes what you and Olga discovered and how you discovered it. Use *I* or *me* in each sentence.

Grade 3: Unit 6   Pronouns   *(Use with pupil book pages 222–223.)*
Skill: Students will use *I* and *me* correctly.

**WORKBOOK PLUS
TCAP PRACTICE**   **109**

Name _____

5 Possessive Pronouns

Possessive Nouns	Possessive Pronouns
Meg's camera is small.	**Her** camera is small.
Meg went to Jay's party.	Meg went to **his** party.
Meg took the guests' pictures.	Meg took **their** pictures.

A Write the possessive pronoun in each sentence.

1. Is that your new camera? _____

2. It is different from my camera. _____

3. George Eastman invented his new camera in 1888. _____

4. Our cameras don't look like Eastman's cameras. _____

5. Dorothea Lange is my favorite photographer. _____

6. Many of her pictures are famous. _____

B Write each sentence. Use a possessive pronoun to take the place of the underlined word or words.

7. There are cameras in Franco and Abe's home.

_____

8. Franco takes pictures of Franco's pet turtle.

_____

9. Some pictures show the turtle in the turtle's shell.

_____

10. Millie's favorite picture shows the turtle walking.

_____

11. Abe takes pictures of Abe's pets too.

_____

12. Abe also takes pictures of Suzanne's puppies.

_____

(continued)

Grade 3: Unit 6 Pronouns (Use with pupil book pages 224–225.)
Skill: Students will identify possessive pronouns and will use them to replace possessive nouns.

Name _____

5 Possessive Pronouns (continued from page 110)

Challenge

Write each group of words another way. Use a possessive pronoun.

1. the camera that belongs to me   _____

2. Jan's and Irv's smiles   _____

3. the camera's strap   _____

4. the film that belongs to you   _____

5. Leo's pictures   _____

6. Margaret's job   _____

7. photos that belong to Dad and me   _____

Look at the words you wrote in the answers above. Each word is hidden in the camera puzzle below. Circle these words. They are written across and down.

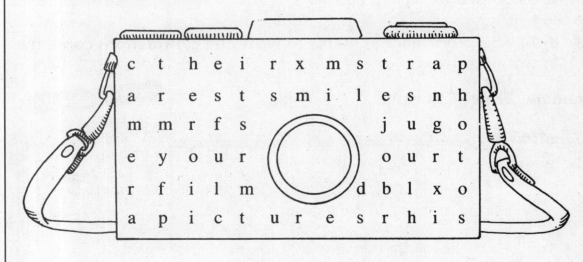

Writing Application: Photo Captions ————————————

    You have a new camera. You have brought it to a birthday party in your class. Think of five pictures you might take at this party. Write a sentence to describe each one. Use a possessive pronoun in each sentence.

Grade 3: Unit 6 Pronouns (Use with pupil book pages 224–225.)
  Skill: Students will use possessive pronouns correctly.

WORKBOOK PLUS
TCAP PRACTICE

111

6 Contractions

Two Words	Contraction
I have played computer games.	**I've** played computer games.
We will play one together.	**We'll** play one together.
You are winning!	**You're** winning!

A Write the contractions for the underlined words.

1. <u>We have</u> talked about computers with Ms. Yee. _____

2. <u>She is</u> our math and science teacher. _____

3. <u>She has</u> shown us some new computer games. _____

4. <u>I will</u> tell you about one of them. _____

5. <u>It is</u> a game to practice math. _____

6. First, <u>you will</u> try to catch the frogs. _____

7. <u>They have</u> got numbers on them. _____

B 8–14. Use proofreading marks to write the contractions correctly in this note.

Example: ~~Theyre~~ They're a lot of fun.

Proofreading Marks

¶	Indent
∧	Add
↗	Delete
≡	Capital letter
/	Small letter

Proofreading

Dear Mom and Dad,

For my birthday, Id like a computer game.

Im sure itll be fun for everyone. Ive already seen the game

I want. Its like the one Rob has. Hes very happy with it. Well

be happy with it too.

Your son,
Glenn

(continued)

Grade 3: Unit 6   Pronouns   *(Use with pupil book pages 226–227.)*
Skill: Students will form contractions from pronouns and verbs.

Name _____

6 Contractions (continued from page 112)

Challenge

The computer screen below shows a game about contractions. Find the contraction in each sentence. Decide what letter or letters have been left out to make each contraction. Write the letters on the frogs.

1. _____ I'll play Funny Frogs with you.

2. _____ You're going to catch the frogs.

3. _____ I'm good at this game.

4. _____ It's fun to play.

5. _____ We'll have trouble catching those frogs.

6. _____ They're so fast!

7. _____ He's caught a frog.

8. _____ No, it's jumped away.

Now complete this sentence. Write the letters from the frogs in the correct spaces below. You will have to capitalize three letters.

_____ nk   _____ · t   me   _____ nd   _____   _____ ll

　　1　　　　2　　　　　　　3　　　4　　　5

l _____ ugh.　　　_____ ,　　_____ !

　6　　　　　　7　　　8

Writing Application: An Advertisement

Suppose that you have invented a new computer game. Write an advertisement for this game. Describe how the game is played and why people should buy it. Use five contractions that are made with pronouns.

© Houghton Mifflin Harcourt Publishing Company

Grade 3: Unit 6 Pronouns *(Use with pupil book pages 226–227.)*
Skill: Students will use contractions made with pronouns.

WORKBOOK PLUS
TCAP PRACTICE

113

7 Using *there*, *their*, and *they're*

> We are going **there** to see Tony and Roma.
> We will go in **their** car.
> **They're** picking us up soon.

A Write *there*, *their*, or *they're* to complete each sentence.

1. Tony and Roma invited us to _____ dance class.

2. We went _____ on Friday.

3. First, we met _____ dance teacher.

4. _____ very fond of her.

5. Chairs were _____ in the corner.

6. _____ for visitors to sit comfortably.

7. We sat _____ and watched.

8. Tony and Roma did _____ lessons well.

9. _____ very good dancers.

B 10–15. Use proofreading marks to correct six pronouns in this invitation.

Example: <u>There</u> sending invitations. *They're*

Proofreading Marks

¶	Indent
∧	Add
ب	Delete
≡	Capital letter
/	Small letter

Proofreading

They're is going to be a dance on Friday.

Tony and Roma will teach there dances to everyone their.

There such good dancers! Their will be plenty of food. So be

sure to be they're.

(continued)

Grade 3: Unit 6 Pronouns *(Use with pupil book pages 228–229.)*
Skill: Students will use *there*, *their*, and *they're* correctly.

7 Using *there*, *their*, and *they're* (continued from page 114)

Challenge

The students in the dance class are practicing for a dance program. Look at the picture. Then write answers to the questions. Use the word *there*, *their*, or *they're* in each answer.

1. Who is teaching the dance class?

_____

2. Where are the children standing?

_____

3. What are the children wearing?

_____

4. Where is the dance class being taught?

_____

5. Are all of the children paying attention to the teacher?

_____

Writing Application: An Invitation ────────── INFORMING

Suppose that you are a dance teacher. You want to invite parents and friends to your students' dance program. Write an invitation to the program. Describe the dances that the students will perform. Use the words *there*, *their*, and *they're* in your invitation.

Grade 3: Unit 6 Pronouns *(Use with pupil book pages 228–229.)*
Skill: Students will use *there*, *their*, and *they're* correctly.

WORKBOOK PLUS
TCAP PRACTICE   **115**

Homophones

> your
> You have one heart in ~~you're~~ body. ~~Its~~ It's important to take care of it.

1–10. Change each underlined homophone to the correct homophone. Use words from the Word Box.

Homophone	Meaning	Homophone	Meaning
pear	fruit	he'll	contraction of *he will*
pair	two of a kind		
heard	past of *hear*	heal	to get better
herd	group of animals	heel	part of a shoe
two	one more than 1	rode	past of *ride*
too	very much	road	a street
to	part of a verb	sail	be on a boat
write	use a pen or pencil	sale	selling something
		they're	contraction of *they are*
right	correct; opposite of *left*	there	opposite of *here*

Revising

My mom lived on a farm. She had everything <u>write</u> <u>they're</u> in her own back

yard. She picked fruit from the <u>pair</u> trees. Milk came from their <u>heard</u> of cows.

In summer, they opened a farm stand. Mom would <u>right</u> the prices on

signs. When they had a <u>sail</u>, she would say, "Ask Dad if <u>heal</u> make a big sign."

Then she would stand by the <u>rode</u> and sell the fruits and vegetables. When

it was <u>two</u> hot <u>too</u> stand, Grandma would bring Mom a chair and some

icy lemonade.

Grade 3: Unit 6 Pronouns *(Use with pupil book page 230.)*
Skill: Students will replace incorrect homophones with correct ones.

Name _____

Supporting Sentences

A paragraph that tells a story is a **narrative paragraph**. It often has a lead sentence, supporting sentences, and a closing sentence. **Supporting sentences** support the main idea by giving details about it. They answer one or more of these questions: *Who? What? Where? When? Why? How?* They help readers use their five senses to feel they are part of the story.

Complete a narrative paragraph about this picture. Read the lead sentence below. Then find details in the picture to support the main idea in the lead sentence. Then write three supporting sentences, using the details.

It takes a lot of hard work to put on a play, but it was all worth it.

_____

_____

_____

_____

_____

_____

_____

_____

The applause at the end made the whole cast and crew feel like stars!

Name _____

Organizing Your Narrative

Weak Organization	Strong Organization
Finally, we drove to our new home in Florida.	First, we packed clothes, books, and toys.
First, we packed clothes, books, and toys.	Then we said goodbye to our friends.
~~Daytona is near the beach.~~	Finally, we drove to our new home in Florida.
Then we said goodbye to our friends.	

Three events for a personal narrative are underlined below. Number each event 1, 2, or 3 to show the order in which it happened. Cross out any details that do not keep to the topic. Then organize the main events and the supporting details in the chart below.

Event _____
<u>gathering materials</u>
ice skating on the
    frozen pond
making invitations
buying film for camera

Event _____
<u>planning the party</u>
picking a date
losing a tooth
making guest list

Event _____
<u>surprising my friend</u>
hiding in closet
yelling "Surprise!"
buying snacks and
    juice

Topic	Main Events	Details
a surprise party for a friend	1.	
	2.	
	3.	

Grade 3: Unit 7 Personal Narrative (Use with pupil book page 271.)
Skill: Students will arrange the main events of a personal narrative in chronological order and choose supporting details for each event.

UNIT 7 PERSONAL NARRATIVE

© Houghton Mifflin Harcourt Publishing Company

Good Beginnings

Weak Beginning	Strong Beginning: Ask a Question
My story is about the time my grandparents came to visit.	What's the best part about having your grandparents come for a visit?

Weak Beginning	Strong Beginning: Set the Scene
My story tells about the arrival of my little sister.	We hung the "Welcome" banner and put balloons all over the house. My new sister from China was coming to live with us.

Each beginning of a personal narrative below needs to be stronger. First, read the story. Then write a stronger beginning, using the strategy suggested.

1. This is a story about the first time I went on an airplane. We were going to my cousin's wedding across the country. I was very scared of flying.

   Ask a Question: _____
   _____
   _____
   _____
   _____

2. My story tells about how I learned to swim. We were at my friend's cabin at Lake George. The lake was dark green and very cold. There were tall pine trees all around.

   Set the Scene: _____
   _____
   _____
   _____
   _____

Grade 3: Unit 7 Personal Narrative (Use with pupil book page 272.)
   Skill: Students will write strong beginnings for personal
   narratives, using two different strategies.

WORKBOOK PLUS
TCAP PRACTICE

119

Writing with Voice

Weak Voice	Strong Voice
Our teacher asked us to bring in lots of boxes and tubes. I wondered what we would do. Then we made robots. I was surprised.	The classroom was filled with boxes and tubes. There were little boxes and huge boxes! There were tiny tubes and very long tubes. What could we be doing with all this stuff? "We are going to make robots!" our teacher said. "Yes!" we all shouted.

The personal narrative below is dull because it does not have a strong voice. Rewrite the narrative to give it a stronger voice. Use words and details that make the personal narrative sound like you.

Cook for a Day

Last week, my mother asked me to cook dinner for the family. I decided to make tacos and salad and fruit. It was easy. I opened the can of beans and put some on each taco shell. Then I warmed up the tacos. When they were warm, I put shredded cheese on top. I put some lettuce and tomatoes in a bowl. Then I put some grapes on a plate. Everyone thought my dinner was good.

Grade 3: Unit 7   Personal Narrative   (Use with pupil book page 273.)
Skill: Students will rewrite a personal narrative to give it a strong voice.

Good Endings

Weak Ending	Strong Ending: How Things Worked Out
My sister cut my brother's hair. It looked bad.	My mother almost fainted when she saw what my sister had done to my brother's hair. The bottom was all raggy. He even had bald patches. When we stopped staring, my mother started to laugh. "It will grow back," she said, "but don't ever do this again!"

Weak Ending	Strong Ending: Sharing Feelings
My team won the science fair. The end.	"You won!" my teacher cheered. We took first prize in the science fair! All our hard work paid off. We all felt proud.

Each short narrative below needs an ending. First, read the story. Then write two endings for each one, using the strategies above. Read your story endings. Put a check mark in front of the one you like better.

1.   "I'm too big for a babysitter!" I told my parents, but Tina the babysitter changed my mind. She was so much fun. First, we played board games. Then Tina showed me how to pop corn, and we watched a movie about apes. Last, Tina taught me how to play a string game called Cat's Cradle.

   Strong Ending: _____

   _____

   Strong Ending: _____

   _____

2.   What would you bring to a multicultural fair? Our teacher said we could bring a food or a family object. First, I wanted to bring a noodle and sour cream dish we call "kugel." Then I wanted to bring a book that my grandfather brought from Germany. The words are all in German, and the pictures are very colorful.

   Strong Ending: _____

   _____

   Strong Ending: _____

   _____

Grade 3: Unit 7   Personal Narrative   *(Use with pupil book page 274.)*
   Skill: Students will write two different endings for personal narratives and then pick the stronger ending.

WORKBOOK PLUS
TCAP PRACTICE   121

Name _____

Revising a Personal Narrative

Have I   **yes**
- written a beginning that asks a question or sets the scene?   ❑
- used only important events and put them in an order that
  makes sense?   ❑
- used details that tell what the writer saw, heard, or felt?   ❑
- used words that sound like me telling the story?   ❑

Revise the following personal narrative to make it better. Use the checklist above to help you. Check off each box when you have finished your revision. Use the spaces between the lines and around the paragraph to make your changes.

Let's Dance

It was exciting when Dad won the big prize on the

game show. Mom and I were in the audience. She had on

a new dress. The host was asking really tough questions,

but Dad kept answering one after another. Every time

Dad gave a correct answer, I got excited. Dad's points

kept adding up. Finally, the announcer asked the last

question. I held my breath. Mom and I were so happy we

danced right into the aisle and right up onto the stage.

Dad got the right answer. Dad put his arms around us and

danced too. I never thought dancing with my parents

could be so much fun!

Name _____

Sentence Fluency

| Two sentences | We saw a parade. We stopped to watch it. |
| Combined with *and* | We saw a parade, and we stopped to watch it. |

Revise the following personal narrative to make it better. Combine the underlined sentences using *and*. Write the revised narrative on the lines below.

It was a cold February afternoon. I was really bored. School was over. I had done my homework. I could not go outside, because it was sleeting. Soon, the wires were covered in ice. The streets were slick.

"Don't get into trouble!" my mother called.

I plugged in my video game. The lights went out! I looked outside. All the lights were out!

"Because of the sleet, the wires are down," my mother said.

I was glad that I hadn't caused the blackout!

_____

_____

_____

_____

_____

_____

_____

_____

_____

_____

_____

_____

Grade 3: Unit 7   Personal Narrative   *(Use with pupil book page 277.)*
Skill: Students will revise a personal narrative by combining
simple sentences to create compound sentences.

WORKBOOK PLUS
TCAP PRACTICE
123

Name _____

Characters and Setting

Character Without Details
Jake left the field.

Character Details
Eight-year-old Jake slammed down the bat and stormed off the field, too angry to speak.

Setting Without Details
It was winter.

Setting Details
It was a cold, cold night in February. The wind blew fiercely, sending needles of ice into my skin.

Write some character and setting details to describe what you see in this picture. Include details that tell what the characters look like, how they act, and how they feel. Write details that tell when the event takes place. Tell what the characters see and hear.

Strong character details: _____

_____

_____

_____

Strong setting details: _____

_____

_____

_____

_____

Grade 3: Unit 8   Story   *(Use with pupil book pages 298–299.)*
Skill: Students will generate details about characters and setting in a story.

UNIT 8 STORY

Planning the Plot

Every story has a **beginning,** a **middle,** and an **end.**

Beginning	Middle	End
Introduces the characters, the setting, and a problem	Shows how the characters deal with the problem	Shows how the problem works out

Look at the pictures of a museum adventure. What story could you write about them? Think about the characters, the setting, and the problem that you would write about. Complete the story map.

The beginning introduces the characters, the setting, and a problem. →

The middle shows how the characters deal with the problem. →

The end shows how the problem works out. →

Beginning

Middle

End

Grade 3: Unit 8   Story   *(Use with pupil book page 300.)*
   Skill: Students will plan a story.

WORKBOOK PLUS
TCAP PRACTICE

125

Name _____

Developing the Plot

Strong Beginnings		
Describe a Character	**Describe the Setting**	**Describe an Action**
Pip fluffed his feathers and paraded across the farmyard.	It was so dry that clouds of dust swirled in the air.	The baby laughed at the bright lights.

Without Dialogue	With Dialogue
The crabs were afraid of the whale. The lobster offered to help.	"The whale will eat us for sure," the crabs said. "I will hide you," the lobster said.

The story below needs a strong beginning, some dialogue, and an ending that tells how the problem is solved. Read the story, and then add a beginning, dialogue, and an ending.

Slipping and Sliding

I was happy to help Dad at the ice arena. He drives the Zamboni, which cleans and smoothes the ice. Dad wanted me to open and close the doors so that he could drive the Zamboni on and off the ice.

As soon as Dad pulled out, I slipped right after him. Without skates, I couldn't get up. I was face down on the ice and soaked. Dad would be driving the Zamboni right back through the doors. Finally, I had an idea.

Strong beginning: _____

_____

_____

Dialogue: _____

_____

_____

Strong ending: _____

_____

_____

Grade 3: Unit 8   Story   (Use with pupil book pages 301–302.)
Skill: Students will write a strong beginning, dialogue, and a strong ending.

Revising a Story

Have I   **yes**

- written a new beginning that catches my audience's interest? ❑
- introduced the characters, the setting, and the problem? ❑
- showed how the characters solved the problem? ❑
- put the events in an order that makes sense? ❑
- used details and dialogue to bring the story to life? ❑

Revise the following story to make it better. Use the checklist above to help you. Check off each box when you have finished your revision. You can use the spaces between the lines and around the story to make your changes.

Lots of Stuffed Animals

Angie's mom thinks Angie has too many stuffed animals. Mom told Angie to get rid of some.

"How can I do that, Mom? I like them all," Angie said.

Then Angie asked if she could keep some animals in the guest room at Grandma's house. Grandma thought it was a great idea. So, the next day Angie and her mom brought some stuffed animals over to Grandma's house.

"That looks nice," said Angie. "Now I'm not so stuffed up anymore!"

Grade 3: Unit 8 Story *(Use with pupil book page 303.)*
    Skill: Students will revise a story, using a revision checklist.

WORKBOOK PLUS
TCAP PRACTICE   127

Name _____

Sentence Fluency

Stringy sentence	The squirrel hopped on the roof and looked around and jumped down.
Smoother sentences	The squirrel hopped on the roof and looked around. Then it jumped down.

The story below has some stringy sentences. They are underlined. Revise the story by breaking the stringy sentences into shorter sentences. Rewrite the story with the new sentences.

Soup's On!

Bernie Bear wanted to have a party and invite all his friends and serve food. First came Rachel Rabbit. She had some carrot soup. Then came the dogs. They had some beef soup and they carried a jug of chicken soup and they gave Bernie hot lamb soup. "Thank you," said Bernie.

Next the gerbils rang the doorbell. They gave Bernie a pot of cold lettuce soup and they handed Bernie a can of bean soup and put down a bowl of green pea soup. Bernie thought, "We will soon be swimming in soup!"

_____

_____

_____

_____

_____

_____

_____

_____

_____

_____

_____

Grade 3: Unit 8 Story (Use with pupil book page 305.)
Skill: Students will revise stringy sentences in a story.

Name _____

Supporting Sentences

Informational paragraphs have a topic sentence, supporting sentences, and a closing sentence. **Supporting sentences** give details and facts about the topic. The supporting sentences are arranged in an order that makes sense.

Look at the picture below and complete the informational paragraph. Read the topic sentence and the closing sentence. Find details in the picture to support the main idea in the topic sentence. Write three supporting sentences, using those details.

◄ **Stegosaurus had heavy armor and ate shrubs and ferns.**

▲ **Tyrannosaurus—the most famous meat-eating dinosaur**

▲ **Ultrasaurus was more than 100 feet long and 60 feet tall.**

What were the dinosaurs like? _____

_____

_____

_____

_____

_____

_____

_____

_____

Even though the dinosaurs are not around anymore, we are still discovering new dinosaur facts.

Grade 3: Section 2   Explaining and Informing   (*Use with pupil book pages 321–325.*)
Skill: Students will complete an informational paragraph with supporting sentences.

WORKBOOK PLUS
TCAP PRACTICE

129

Name _____

Organizing Your Instructions

Put Steps in the Right Order	Use Order Words
1. Boil 6 ounces of water.	*first, second, third*
2. Stir in cocoa powder.	*next, finally*
3. Add two spoons of milk.	*then, now*

What steps do you follow when you get ready for school in the morning? Suppose you are teaching a younger child to get ready for school. Number the pictures in the order the steps should be done. Part of a Steps Chart is shown below. List your steps, using order words.

Steps

© Houghton Mifflin Harcourt Publishing Company

UNIT 9 INSTRUCTIONS

130 WORKBOOK PLUS
TCAP PRACTICE

Grade 3: Unit 9   Instructions   *(Use with pupil book page 336.)*
Skill: Students will organize the steps for instructions.

Using Details

Without Exact Details	With Exact Details
Add the dog shampoo.	Wet your dog. Put a teaspoon of dog shampoo in your hand. Gently rub the shampoo on your dog. Start with head, and work down to legs.

Complete these instructions for getting dressed when the weather is bad. Read the opening sentence below. Next, find details in the pictures. Write four steps in the directions.

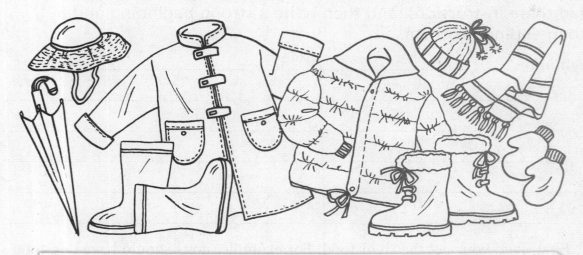

It takes a lot of time to get dressed when the weather is bad.

First, _____

_____

Then, _____

_____

Next, _____

_____

Finally, _____

_____

Grade 3: Unit 9   Instructions   (Use with pupil book page 337.)
   Skill: Students will add details to their instructions.

WORKBOOK PLUS
TCAP PRACTICE   **131**

Good Beginnings and Endings

Weak Beginning	Strong Beginning
This is how you skate.	In-line skating is easy if you follow these simple directions.

Weak Ending	Strong Ending
Now you know how to skate.	Just wait until you zoom down the street on your skates. Don't forget your safety gear!

Every set of instructions needs a strong beginning and ending. Read these instructions, and then write a strong beginning and a strong ending for them.

Beginning: _____

_____

_____

_____

_____

. . . First, feed your pet the right food. For example, dogs should have dog food, not table scraps. Rabbits like lettuce and other shredded vegetables. Next, keep your pet's space or cage clean. You can put newspapers on the bottom of a birdcage to catch droppings. Throw the papers out every other day. Take your dog for walks at least three times a day. Finally, give your pet love. Cuddle your cat and pet your dog.

Ending: _____

_____

_____

_____

_____

_____

132 WORKBOOK PLUS
TCAP PRACTICE

Grade 3: Unit 9 Instructions *(Use with pupil book page 338.)*
Skill: Students will write a strong beginning and ending for instructions.

Revising Instructions

Have I   **yes**
- written a beginning that tells in an interesting way what the instructions are about?   ❑
- included all the steps and listed all the needed materials?   ❑
- put all the steps in the correct order and used order words?   ❑
- used details to make each step clear?   ❑
- written an ending to make the instructions feel finished?   ❑

Revise the following instructions to make them better. Use the checklist above to help you. Check off each box when you have finished your revision. Use the spaces between the lines and around the paragraph to make your changes.

Pigs in Blankets

It is fun to make these snacks. First, get one hot dog, one slice of white bread, a dull knife, a rolling pin, and some foil. Next, preheat the oven to 350º. You'll need adult help with the knife and the oven.

Third, cut off the four crusty edges of the bread. Then use the rolling pin to roll the bread until it is thin and flat. Next, cut the bread into three long strips. Next, put a piece of hot dog onto a strip of bread and roll up the bread around the hot dog. Cut the hot dog into three pieces. Put all the pieces on the foil and bake for 5 minutes.

Grade 3: Unit 9 Instructions *(Use with pupil book page 339.)*
Skill: Students will revise instructions, using a revision checklist.

WORKBOOK PLUS
TCAP PRACTICE   **133**

Elaborating: Word Choice

Without Exact Verbs	With Exact Verbs
Move slowly when you get on the ice.	Glide slowly when you get on the ice.

Practice your revising skills by filling in this chart. Add exact verbs to each step. Write your answers on the lines.

Without Exact Verbs	With Exact Verbs
Put a thin coat of glue on the cardboard.	_____ a thin coat of glue on the cardboard.
Put your magazine picture on the sticky paper.	_____ your magazine picture on the sticky paper.
When it's dry, cut the edges of the puzzle.	When it's dry, _____ the edges of the puzzle.v
Make four lines on the back of the puzzle.	_____ four lines on the back of the puzzle.
Cut the puzzle pieces apart.	_____ the puzzle pieces apart.
Put your puzzle pieces in an envelope.	_____ your puzzle pieces in an envelope.

Grade 3: Unit 9 Instructions (Use with pupil book page 341.)
Skill: Students will revise a set of instructions using exact verbs.

Gathering Facts

Facts	Opinions
On April 6, 1909, Matthew Henson reached the North Pole.	The North Pole is an interesting place.
Henson was 42 years old.	I think Henson was brave.
He spoke the language of the Inuit people.	Foreign languages are important.

These are questions you might ask if you were writing a research report. Each question is followed by a fact and an opinion. Choose the fact and write it on the line.

1. Why is Abraham Lincoln important in United States history?

Abraham Lincoln was President during the Civil War.

Abraham Lincoln is the most famous United States President.

_____

2. How are cucumbers and tomatoes alike?

I love salads with cucumber and tomatoes.

Cucumber and tomatoes grow on vines.

_____

3. What is the object of the game of basketball?

Basketball players wear the coolest uniforms.

Players score points by throwing a ball through a hoop.

_____

4. What skills do you need to play video games?

Video games call for concentration and quick reflexes.

I think that everyone enjoys video games.

_____

Grade 3: Unit 10   Research Report   *(Use with pupil book pages 366–367.)*
Skill: Students will distinguish between facts and opinions.

WORKBOOK PLUS
TCAP PRACTICE

135

Name _____

Good Openings and Closings

Weak Opening
I'm going to tell you all about storms.

Strong Openings	
Interesting Fact	**Question**
A thunderstorm is more powerful than a bulldozer.	What is the most dangerous type of storm?

Weak Closing
In this report, I told you all about storms.

Strong Closing
Hurricanes, thunderstorms, and tornadoes are the greatest storms on earth. Next time you hear thunder, think of a storm's great power.

For each report below, write an opening that gives an interesting fact or asks a question. Then write a strong closing that sums up the main ideas.

Moving bits of cloud, such as raindrops and hail, can become electrically charged. Lightning is a huge electric spark that flashes when opposite charges flow toward one another. Heat from the lightning causes air to spread out suddenly. The warm air crashes into layers of cooler air around it. This makes the sound we call thunder.

Strong Opening: _____

_____

Strong Closing: _____

_____

The whirling black column of a tornado is called a funnel cloud. The winds inside a funnel cloud spin at 300 miles per hour. The funnel cloud moves along like a giant vacuum cleaner. It picks up cars, houses, and everything in its way. After it has passed, you might see a school of fish in your front yard!

Strong Opening: _____

_____

Strong Closing: _____

_____

136 WORKBOOK PLUS
TCAP PRACTICE

Grade 3: Unit 10   Research Report   *(Use with pupil book page 370.)*
Skill: Students will write strong openings and closings.

Revising a Research Report

Have I
- written a new opening that states the topic in an interesting way?
- included a main idea and supporting details in each paragraph?
- included only facts?
- used my own words?
- summed up the important points?

yes
❑
❑
❑
❑
❑

Revise the following research report to make it better. Use the checklist above to help you. Check off each box when you have finished revising. Use the spaces between the lines and around the paragraph to make your changes.

A Song of Violins

An orchestra has more violins than any other

instrument. I think the violin is the nicest instrument.

The violin has four strings that stretch down its body

from its neck and over a bridge. This keeps the strings very

tight. The violinist tucks the bottom of the violin under his

or her chin and holds the neck with one hand. The fingers

of this hand press down on the strings. The other hand

holds the bow.

Violins can play all kinds of music, from classical to

jazz to folk. I like jazz violin.

Grade 3: Unit 10   Research Report   *(Use with pupil book page 371.)*
Skill: Students will revise a research report, using a checklist.

WORKBOOK PLUS
TCAP PRACTICE

137

Name _____

Elaborating: Details

Without details	Trees need a lot of water to survive.
With details	Trees need a lot of water to survive. A large tree absorbs 95 gallons of water every day.

This part of a research report about how trees get their food does not have enough details. Revise the paragraph by adding details from the diagram. Write the revised report on the lines below.

Can you picture yourself eating only sunlight, water, and air? Those are the ingredients trees use to make their food. Roots soak up water. Water travels up the trunk. Air goes into the leaves. The sun shines. Leaves make food for the tree.

Leaves use energy from sun, carbon dioxide from air, and sap to make sugar.

Sap travels up to the leaves.

Roots take water from the soil.

_____

_____

_____

_____

_____

_____

_____

_____

Grade 3: Unit 10   Research Report   *(Use with pupil book page 373.)*
Skill: Students will revise a research report by adding details.

Name _____

Supporting Sentences

A paragraph that gives the writer's point of view is an **opinion paragraph**. It has **supporting sentences** that tell the reasons for the writer's opinion. They help readers understand why the writer feels a certain way about a topic.

Use the picture below to help you complete the opinion paragraph. Read the topic sentence and the concluding sentence. Then find details in the picture to support the main idea. Last, use those details to write three supporting sentences. Be sure the supporting sentences tell the reasons for your opinion.

Allen Park must be fixed up now! _____

_____

_____

_____

_____

_____

_____

_____

By working together we can make our town a better place.

Name _____

Choosing Strong Reasons

Opinion: I do not like grapefruits.

Weak Reasons	Strong Reasons
They taste bad. They are messy.	They taste bitter and sour. The juice squirts on my shirt and in my eye!

Each opinion needs two strong reasons. Read the opinions and write strong reasons that answer the question *Why?* Then circle your strongest reason for each opinion.

1. I like reading because...

Reason 1: _____

_____

Reason 2: _____

_____

2. I do not like to clean my room because...

Reason 1: _____

_____

_____

Reason 2: _____

_____

3. I like winter vacation because...

Reason 1: _____

_____

_____

Reason 2: _____

_____

Grade 3: Unit 11 Opinion *(Use with pupil book pages 399–400.)*
Skill: Students will write strong reasons to support opinions.

UNIT 11 OPINION

Name _____

Elaborating Your Reasons

Opinion: I love camping!

Weak Details	Strong Details
have fun	hike in the woods, cook over the campfire
see animals	bears, raccoons, squirrels

Each reason needs strong details. Read the reasons below. Then add strong details that will help your readers understand the reasons.

Opinion: I like my dog Skippy because...

Reason: Skippy and I have fun together.

Detail: _____

Detail: _____

Detail: _____

Opinion: I like holidays because...

Reason: I get to have fun with all my relatives.

Detail: _____

Detail: _____

Detail: _____

Opinion: I like going to the city because...

Reason: I do things that are lots of fun.

Detail: _____

Detail: _____

Detail: _____

© Houghton Mifflin Harcourt Publishing Company

Grade 3: Unit 11 Opinion *(Use with pupil book pages 401–402.)*
  Skill: Students will write strong details to support reasons for an opinion.

WORKBOOK PLUS
TCAP PRACTICE
141

Good Openings and Closings

Weak Opening	Strong Opening
There are many reasons I like going to the town pool.	Splash! I'm the first one in the cool blue pool. It's a great place to be on a hot day.

Weak Closing	Strong Closing
That is why I like to go to the town pool.	At the pool, I can dive into the cool water, swim with my friends, and play games.

Every opinion essay needs a strong opening and closing. Read this essay and then write a good opening and closing for it.

One reason I like stuffed toys is that they are pretty. I like my plush purple hippo, fuzzy red bear, and bright green parrot. Stuffed toys are also fun to trade. I made friends with Kate and Brandon trading our toys at a swap meet. Stuffed toys can be worth a lot of money. I paid $6 for a small tiger and sold it for $10. Then I put the extra money in my bank to save up for another stuffed toy.

Strong opening: _____

_____

_____

_____

_____

Strong closing: _____

_____

_____

_____

_____

_____

Grade 3: Unit 11 Opinion *(Use with pupil book page 404.)*
Skill: Students will write a strong opening and closing
for an opinion essay.

Revising an Opinion Essay

Have I   **yes**
- introduced the topic in an interesting way?   ❑
- used a topic sentence to state each reason?   ❑
- given strong reasons for the opinion?   ❑
- supported the reasons with details?   ❑
- summarized the main points in the closing?   ❑

Revise the following opinion essay. Use the checklist above to help you. Check off each box when you have finished revising. Use the spaces between the lines and around the essay to make your changes.

Fun on the Farm

Visiting my cousin's farm is my favorite thing to do. I never get bored when I am there. It's fun to get up early and watch the sun rise. That's also when we feed the chickens.

In the afternoons, we like to go for a swim in the pond. If it's winter, we go ice-skating on the pond.

Working with the horses is the most fun.

Before we know it, bedtime rolls around. My cousin and I talk in the dark before we fall asleep.

Grade 3: Unit 11   Opinion   *(Use with pupil book page 405.)*
Skill: Students will revise an opinion essay, using a revision checklist.

WORKBOOK PLUS
TCAP PRACTICE   143

Name _____

Elaborating: Word Choice

Without synonyms	I love to play **games**. I play **games** with my sister and I play **games** with my friends.
With synonyms	I love to play **games**. I play **checkers** with my sister and I play **hopscotch** with my friends.

Revise these opinion sentences by replacing two of the underlined words in each set with synonyms to make your writing more interesting. Write your new sentences on the lines.

I like to play with <u>big</u> dogs. My dog is <u>big</u>. It is fun to roll in the grass with a <u>big</u> dog.

_____

_____

_____

_____

That <u>child</u> is the best swimmer I know. That <u>child</u> took lessons at the village pool. For a <u>child</u>, he is very fast.

_____

_____

_____

_____

This <u>plant</u> is the nicest one in our house. The <u>plant</u> is easy to take care of. It is also Mom's favorite <u>plant</u>.

_____

_____

_____

_____

144 WORKBOOK PLUS
TCAP PRACTICE

Grade 3: Unit 11   Opinion   *(Use with pupil book page 407.)*
Skill: Students will revise sentences by adding synonyms.

Supporting Your Reasons

Reason: Our school should have cooking classes so we can learn how to help more at home.

Weak Support	Strong Support	
Opinion	**Fact**	**Example**
I think learning how to cook is really neat.	A survey of our school showed that 212 students are interested in learning to cook.	I would be able to make lunch on Saturdays so my parents could rest more.

Read the following reasons. Then write a fact and an example to support each one.

1. Our town needs a new library because the old one is too small.

   Fact: _____

   _____

   _____

   Example: _____

   _____

   _____

2. The zoo needs more volunteers to help the staff care for the animals.

   Fact: _____

   _____

   _____

   Example: _____

   _____

   _____

Grade 3: Unit 12   Persuasion   *(Use with pupil book pages 434–435.)*
   Skill: Students will write strong facts and examples to support reasons.

WORKBOOK PLUS
TCAP PRACTICE

145

Name _____

Organizing Your Essay

We need a sign-up system for using the computers.
2 We spend too much time deciding whose turn it is.
~~Computer games are cool.~~
3 The teacher would know who uses the computer.
1 A system would make sure everybody gets a turn.

Listed below are four reasons that might appear in a persuasive essay. Cross out the reason that does not stick to the topic. Number the other reasons to show the order in which they should be given. Then write the reasons in the correct order on the lines below. Last, add a fact or example for each reason.

Goal: Our town needs a park.

_____ Also, bigger kids need a place to play baseball and soccer.

_____ In the first place, little kids need swings, sandboxes, and climbing toys.

_____ Finally, we have five acres by the library that are not being used.

_____ There is a great park in Conway.

Reason #1: _____

_____

Fact or Example: _____

_____

Reason #2: _____

_____

Fact or Example: _____

_____

Reason #3: _____

_____

Fact or Example: _____

_____

Grade 3: Unit 12 Persuasion *(Use with pupil book page 436.)*
Skill: Students will organize reasons for a persuasive essay and supply missing details.

Good Openings and Closings

Weak Opening
Main Street isn't pretty. There aren't any flowers. I think we should have flowers on Main Street.

Strong Opening
Welcome to Main Street! Don't you want people to like our town? Kids and grown-ups should plant flowers on Main Street every spring.

Weak Closing
When I go to Main Street, I don't see any flowers. I see lots of flowers in front of the school.

Strong Closing
If everyone gets together and plants flowers on Main Street in May and June, our town will be beautiful. More people will shop in town, eat dinner there, and go to concerts.

The openings and closings below are weak.
Read each one and then write a strong opening
and a strong closing.

1. **Weak Opening:** I want a pet so I can do stuff with it.

   Strong Opening: _____

   _____

   _____

   Weak Closing: It's good to do stuff with a pet.

   Strong Closing: _____

   _____

2. **Weak Opening:** A swap meet is a good way to get rid of things.

   Strong Opening: _____

   _____

   _____

   Weak Closing: Let's have a swap meet so I can have fun.

   Strong Closing: _____

   _____

Grade 3: Unit 12   Persuasion   *(Use with pupil book page 437.)*
    Skill: Students will write strong openings and closings for persuasive essays.

WORKBOOK PLUS
TCAP PRACTICE

147

Writing with Voice

Weak Voice
A field day would be a good idea. We would all have fun. We could run around and play nice games.

Strong Voice
Batter up! At field day, we could play baseball and have relay races. Wouldn't some ice-cold watermelon taste great too?

Angry Voice
I have to decorate my own room so it will look good. If I don't, my room will be awful. I won't like it because it will look babyish.

Positive Voice
If I could decorate my own room, I would paint the walls light blue and hang stars from the ceiling. My room would look so great that I'd keep it clean all the time!

The persuasive essay below sounds angry and whiny. Put yourself in the writer's place and then rewrite the essay, using a strong, positive voice.

If we can't sell candy during lunch, we'll never have any fun! We won't be able to go on any field trips to museums. We'll get stuck with the same junky playground toys. They have been broken for ages, and nobody wants to play on them. We won't even get a party at the end of the year. We need to sell the candy.

_____
_____
_____
_____
_____
_____
_____
_____
_____
_____
_____

Grade 3: Unit 12 Persuasion *(Use with pupil book page 438.)*
Skill: Students will rewrite a persuasive essay, adding their own individual voice.

Revising a Persuasive Essay

Have I	yes
• written a new opening that tells the goal in an interesting way?	❏
• used facts and examples to support the reasons?	❏
• made the writing sound positive and sound like my voice?	❏
• revised the closing to sum up the goals and reasons?	❏

Revise the following persuasive essay to make it better. Use the checklist above to help you. Check off each box when you have finished revising. Use the spaces between the lines and around the essay to make your changes.

Our school library needs to get on the Internet. We are lucky to have a computer there, but it needs to do more. If that computer had Internet access, we could do more research for our schoolwork.

Internet access on the library computer would also let us contact other students in other schools all over the world. That would help us learn more about customs and traditions everywhere.

Let's get the school library on the Internet now!

Grade 3: Unit 12 Persuasion *(Use with pupil book page 439.)*
Skill: Students will revise a persuasive essay, using a revision checklist.

WORKBOOK PLUS
TCAP PRACTICE

149

Name _____

Sentence Fluency

Not a complete sentence	We should go to the park later. Because there will be fireworks after dark.
Complete sentence	We should go to the park later because there will be fireworks after dark.

Read this paragraph from a persuasive essay. Rewrite the paragraph, fixing any incomplete sentences you find.

I think the hiking group should go on a camping trip. Since we have two days off from school. We could hike along the lake and then camp in the hills. I can carry the food. Because I have the largest backpack. Chang can watch for animals. Since he has good binoculars. This could be the best trip of the year. Because we all like to hike and camp out in the woods.

_____

_____

_____

_____

_____

_____

_____

_____

_____

Grade 3: Unit 12   Persuasion   *(Use with pupil book page 441.)*
Skill: Students will revise a persuasive essay by creating complete sentences.

TCAP Practice

Tennessee Topics

Monday

1 <u>**Luke visited the Great Smokies he hiked up a park trail.**</u> **is a run-on sentence. How could it be rewritten to make complete and correctly written sentences?**

Ⓐ Luke visited the Great Smokies. He hiked up a park trail.

Ⓑ Luke visited. The Great Smokies. He hiked up a park trail.

Ⓒ Luke visited the Great Smokies. He hiked. Up a park trail.

Ⓓ Luke visited the Great Smokies he hiked up. A park trail.

Tuesday

2 **Read the sentence and decide which part, if any, needs a capital letter.**

The park | is not far | from knoxville, Tennessee. | None
   Ⓕ   Ⓖ   Ⓗ   Ⓙ

Wednesday

3 **Choose the** <u>**best**</u> **way to write this sentence.**

People have see bears in the Smokies.

Ⓐ People has see bears in the Smokies.

Ⓑ People have seen bears in the Smokies.

Ⓒ People have saw bears in the Smokies.

Ⓓ Best as it is

Tennessee Topics

Thursday

4 **Decide which punctuation mark, if any, is needed in the sentence.**

Streams flow beside the mountain trails

.   ?   !   None
Ⓕ   Ⓖ   Ⓗ   Ⓙ

Friday

5 **Which sentence is written correctly?**

Ⓐ   Have you ever gone fishing.

Ⓑ   luke and his friend fished in a stream

Ⓒ   They waded into the water.

Ⓓ   Mr. carter caught a trout.

Journal Writing Ideas

- What do you like to do outdoors? Tell why you like it.

- Would you like to go fishing? Explain why or why not.

Tennessee Topics

Monday

1 **Decide which punctuation mark, if any, is needed in the sentence.**

What an exciting city Nashville is

. ? ! None

Ⓐ Ⓑ Ⓒ Ⓓ

Tuesday

2 **Nashville is a big city in Tennessee it is the state capital. is a run-on sentence. How could it be rewritten to make complete and correctly written sentences?**

Ⓕ Nashville is a big city. In Tennessee. It is the state capital.

Ⓖ Nashville is a big city in Tennessee. It is the state capital.

Ⓗ Nashville is a big city. In Tennessee it is. The state capital.

Ⓙ Nashville is. A big city in Tennessee. It is the state capital.

Wednesday

3 **Read the sentence and decide which part, if any, needs a capital letter.**

a state fair | takes place in Nashville | in September. | None

Ⓐ Ⓑ Ⓒ Ⓓ

Tennessee Topics

Thursday

4 **Choose the best way to write this sentence.**

Country bands performs at Nashville's Opryland.

Ⓕ Country bands has performed at Nashville's Opryland.

Ⓖ Country bands is performing at Nashville's Opryland.

Ⓗ Country bands perform at Nashville's Opryland.

Ⓙ Best as it is

Friday

5 **Find the sentence that is complete and written correctly.**

Ⓐ Many large and small businesses in Nashville.

Ⓑ Several companies in the city print books.

Ⓒ Teaching at universities such as Vanderbilt.

Ⓓ Jobs in the music business and in health care.

Journal Writing Ideas

- What is one kind of job people do where you live? What would you like or dislike about doing that job?

- What is something fun or interesting to do in a town or city near you? Tell about the activity.

Tennessee Topics   **Week 3**

Monday

1 **Read the two sentences.**

Tennessee has strawberry festivals.

Tennessee has pumpkin festivals.

What is the best way to combine these sentences?

Ⓐ   Tennessee has strawberry festivals, and Tennessee has pumpkin festivals.

Ⓑ   Tennessee has strawberry and pumpkin festivals.

Ⓒ   Tennessee has strawberry festivals and has pumpkin festivals.

Ⓓ   Tennessee has festivals for strawberries, and Tennessee has festivals for pumpkins.

Tuesday

2 **Tennessee's oldest strawberry festival is not a complete sentence. Which words could be added to make it a complete and correctly written sentence?**

Tennessee's oldest strawberry festival _____.

Ⓕ   in the western part of the state

Ⓗ   for more than 75 years

Ⓖ   every year in May

Ⓙ   takes place in Humbolt

Wednesday

3 **Decide which punctuation mark, if any, is needed in the sentence.**

Which Tennessee town holds a giant pumpkin contest

.   ?   !   None

Ⓐ   Ⓑ   Ⓒ   Ⓓ

© Houghton Mifflin Harcourt Publishing Company

Tennessee Topics

Thursday

4 **Find the sentence that is complete and written correctly.**

- Ⓕ A pumpkin festival in Allardt, Tennessee.
- Ⓖ Giant pumpkins as big as a baby elephant.
- Ⓗ The winning pumpkins weigh hundreds of pounds.
- Ⓙ Grown by farmers and gardeners from several states.

Friday

5 **Read the sentence and decide which part, if any, needs a capital letter.**

Gleason | holds a sweet potato festival | on Labor day. | None

   Ⓐ   Ⓑ   Ⓒ   Ⓓ

Journal Writing Ideas

- What fair or festival have you attended? Tell about what you saw and did.

- Have you ever grown a fruit, vegetable, or other plant? Tell what you did to help it grow. How did it change as it grew?

Tennessee Topics

Monday

1 **Find the sentence that is complete and written correctly.**

- Ⓐ The Tennessee river in the southeastern United States.
- Ⓑ Follows a U-shaped path through three states.
- Ⓒ May have been named after a Cherokee village.
- Ⓓ The Tennessee River provides power for electricity.

Tuesday

2 **Decide which punctuation mark, if any, is needed in the sentence.**

How long is the Tennessee River

.	?	!	None
Ⓕ	Ⓖ	Ⓗ	Ⓙ

Wednesday

3 **Read the sentence and decide which part, if any, needs a capital letter.**

The Tennessee River | winds 652 miles | to the Ohio river. | None

| Ⓐ | Ⓑ | Ⓒ | Ⓓ |

Tennessee Topics

There are a few mistakes in the sign
that need correcting.

 1   The Tennessee River begins
near knoxville, Tennessee.

 2   It flows through Alabama.
It flows through Kentucky.

Thursday

4   **Choose the <u>best</u> way to write part of Number 1 in the sign.**

    Ⓕ   Knoxville, Tennessee

    Ⓖ   knoxville Tennessee

    Ⓗ   Knoxville Tennessee

    Ⓙ   Correct as it is

Friday

5   **What is the <u>best</u> way to combine the sentences in Number 2 in the sign?**

    Ⓐ   It flows through Alabama, and it flows through Kentucky.

    Ⓑ   It flows through Alabama and Kentucky.

    Ⓒ   It flows through Alabama and flows through Kentucky.

    Ⓓ   It flows through Alabama, Kentucky.

Journal Writing Ideas

- What river, ocean, lake, or pond have you seen? Describe the water, land, plants, and animals that you saw.

- Would you like to live near a body of water? Explain why or why not.

Tennessee Topics   Week 5

Monday

1 **Read the sentence and decide which part, if any, needs a capital letter.**

Last week │ i wrote a report │ about Andrew Jackson. │ None
   Ⓐ   Ⓑ   Ⓒ   Ⓓ

Tuesday

2 **Decide which punctuation mark, if any, is needed in the sentence.**

Andrew Jackson was the seventh United States president

   .   ?   !   None
  Ⓕ   Ⓖ   Ⓗ   Ⓙ

Wednesday

3 **Jackson had a farm in Nashville he raised cotton and grain. is a run-on sentence. How could it be rewritten to make complete and correctly written sentences?**

Ⓐ Jackson had a farm. In Nashville. He raised cotton and grain.

Ⓑ Jackson had a farm in Nashville he raised cotton. And grain.

Ⓒ Jackson had a farm in Nashville. He raised cotton and grain.

Ⓓ Jackson had. A farm in Nashville. He raised cotton and grain.

Tennessee Topics

Thursday

4 **Find the sentence that is complete and written correctly.**

- Ⓕ Andrew Jackson's home in Nashville.
- Ⓖ He called it the Hermitage.
- Ⓗ A large brick house and beautiful garden.
- Ⓙ Today a museum for everyone.

Friday

5 **Which sentence is written correctly?**

- Ⓐ Andrew Jackson was elected to the U.S. Senate twice.
- Ⓑ In 1798 he became a judge in Tennessee's highest court
- Ⓒ He was elected president of the United States in 1829?
- Ⓓ I will give my report about Jackson on tuesday.

Journal Writing Ideas

- If you were president of the United States, what would you do to improve your country? Explain why your idea is important.

- Who is a good leader in your school, neighborhood, or home? Why do you think that person is a good leader?

Tennessee Topics

Monday

1 **Decide which punctuation mark, if any, is needed in the sentence.**

Is the Pink Palace in Memphis really a palace

.	?	!	None
Ⓐ	Ⓑ	Ⓒ	Ⓓ

Tuesday

2 **Which sentence is written correctly?**

Ⓕ The Pink Palace's walls was built with pink marble.

Ⓖ The Pink Palace's walls were built with pink marble.

Ⓗ The Pink Palace's walls be built with pink marble.

Ⓙ The Pink Palace's walls is built with pink marble.

Wednesday

3 **Read the sentence and decide which part, if any, needs a capital letter.**

Clarence saunders | built the Pink Palace | as a house. | None

      Ⓐ   Ⓑ   Ⓒ   Ⓓ

Tennessee Topics

Thursday

4 **Find the sentence that is complete and written correctly.**

- Ⓕ Is now the Memphis Pink Palace Museum.
- Ⓖ Teaches about Memphis nature and history.
- Ⓗ Visitors can tour an old-style grocery store.
- Ⓙ A model of an old-fashioned circus.

Friday

5 **Choose the _best_ way to write this sentence.**

Today the Pink Palace Museum has a science center too.

- Ⓐ Today the Pink Palace Museum is having a science center too.
- Ⓑ Today the Pink Palace Museum had a science center too.
- Ⓒ Today the Pink Palace Museum will have a science center too.
- Ⓓ Best as it is

Journal Writing Ideas

- What place have you visited where you learned something interesting? Tell about the place and what you learned.

- One hundred years ago, life in your area was very different than it is today. What are some things that you think were different back then?

Tennessee Topics

Monday

1 **Decide which punctuation mark, if any, is needed in the sentence.**

I went to Graceland last weekend

　. 　 ? 　 ! 　 None

　Ⓐ 　 Ⓑ 　 Ⓒ 　 Ⓓ

Tuesday

2 **Our tour bus is not a complete sentence. Which words could be added to make it a complete and correctly written sentence?**

Our tour bus _____.

Ⓕ to Graceland

Ⓖ were late

Ⓗ was very crowded

Ⓙ driving to Graceland

Wednesday

3 **Read the sentence and decide which part, if any, needs a capital letter.**

Graceland was | the home of | Elvis presley. | None

　Ⓐ 　　　 Ⓑ 　　　 Ⓒ 　　 Ⓓ

Tennessee Topics

Thursday

4 **Don't go to Graceland on Tuesdays in the winter it's closed.** **is a run-on sentence. How could it be rewritten to make complete and correctly written sentences?**

- Ⓕ   Don't go. To Graceland on Tuesdays. In the winter it's closed.
- Ⓖ   Don't go to Graceland on Tuesdays. In the winter. It's closed.
- Ⓗ   Don't go to Graceland on Tuesdays in the winter. It's closed.
- Ⓙ   Don't go. To Graceland on Tuesdays in the winter it's closed.

Friday

5 **Read the two sentences.**

I would like to visit Graceland.

I would like to visit the Memphis Zoo.

What is the best way to combine these sentences?

- Ⓐ   I would like to visit Graceland and the Memphis Zoo.
- Ⓑ   I would like to visit Graceland, and I would like to visit the Memphis Zoo.
- Ⓒ   I would like to visit Graceland and visit the Memphis Zoo.
- Ⓓ   Visiting Graceland and visiting the Memphis Zoo I would like.

Journal Writing Ideas

- Where would you like to go for a vacation? Why?

- Have you been to Graceland? What did you like about it? If you haven't been there, would you like to go? Why or why not?

Tennessee Topics

Monday

1 **Read the sentence and decide which part, if any, needs a capital letter.**

Wilma rudolph | was a great runner | from Tennessee. | None

   (A)   (B)   (C)   (D)

Tuesday

2 **Decide which punctuation mark, if any, is needed in the sentence.**

Young Wilma Rudolph's legs were weak from an illness

  .   ?   !   None

(F)   (G)   (H)   (J)

Wednesday

3 **Find the sentence that is complete and written correctly.**

(A)   As brave and talented as Wilma Rudolph.

(B)   Wilma worked hard to grow strong.

(C)   Broke world records in many races.

(D)   The pride of her hometown, Clarksville.

Tennessee Topics

There are a few mistakes in the sign that need correcting.

	Wilma Rudolph was born on June 23 1940.
	She is known for her speed grace and courage.

Thursday

4 Choose the <u>best</u> way to write part of Number 1 in the sign.

    Ⓕ   june 23, 1940

    Ⓖ   june 23 1940

    Ⓗ   June 23, 1940

    Ⓙ   Correct as it is

Friday

5 Choose the <u>best</u> way to write Number 2 in the sign.

    Ⓐ   She is known for her Grace, Speed and courage.

    Ⓑ   She is known for her grace speed, and courage.

    Ⓒ   She is known for her grace, speed, and courage.

    Ⓓ   Best as it is

Journal Writing Ideas

- Do you like to take part in races? Why or why not?
- What person in sports is a hero to you? Why?

Tennessee Topics

Monday

1 **Which sentence has the correct capitalization and punctuation?**

Ⓐ rowing has become a popular sport in Tennessee.

Ⓑ The state's many rivers helped the sport grow.

Ⓒ Can anyone learn how to row a rowboat.

Ⓓ Madison went rowing with her mom on thursday.

Tuesday

2 **Read the sentence and decide which part, if any, needs a capital letter.**

A rowing race | takes place in october | in Knoxville. | None

    Ⓕ   Ⓖ   Ⓗ   Ⓙ

Wednesday

3 **Which sentence is written correctly?**

Ⓐ A shell is a rowboat used for racing.

Ⓑ Shells is long and narrow.

Ⓒ Some shells has room for eight rowers.

Ⓓ One person steer the boat.

Tennessee Topics

Thursday

4 **Find the sentence that is complete and written correctly.**

- Ⓕ Rowboats in Egypt 4,000 years ago.
- Ⓖ Used for travel and carrying goods in the past.
- Ⓗ People today row for fun and exercise.
- Ⓙ Fresh air, sunshine, water, and teamwork.

Friday

5 **Decide which punctuation mark, if any, is needed in the sentence.**

What a wonderful sport rowing is

.	?	!	None
Ⓐ	Ⓑ	Ⓒ	Ⓓ

Journal Writing Ideas

- Describe a kind of boat that you have seen. Tell what it would be like to go for a ride in that boat.

- What kind of outdoor activity or exercise do you like? Explain why you like it.

Tennessee Topics   **Week 10**

Monday

1 **Read the sentence and decide which part, if any, needs a capital letter.**

Can you tell | me when | thanksgiving Day is? | None

    (A)   (B)   (C)   (D)

Tuesday

2 **Decide which punctuation mark, if any, is needed in the sentence.**

Does your town have a parade every year on Thanksgiving

   .   ?   !   None

 (F)   (G)   (H)   (J)

Wednesday

3 **Read the two sentences.**

Some bands wear uniforms.

Some bands play marches.

What is the <u>best</u> way to combine these sentences?

(A) Some bands wear uniforms, and some bands play marches.

(B) Some bands are wearing uniforms and marching.

(C) Some bands wear uniforms and play marches.

(D) Wear uniforms and play marches.

Tennessee Topics

There are a few mistakes in the sign that need correcting.

> Country Music on Thanksgiving Day!
>
> ▽1   Here your favorite music!
>
> ▽2   Come to nashville!

Thursday

4 Choose the <u>best</u> way to write Number 1 in the sign.

- Ⓕ   hear your favorite music!
- Ⓖ   Here your favorite music?
- Ⓗ   Hear your favorite music!
- Ⓙ   Correct as it is

Friday

5 Choose the <u>best</u> way to write Number 2 in the sign.

- Ⓐ   come to Nashville!
- Ⓑ   Come to Nashville!
- Ⓒ   Come to Nashville?
- Ⓓ   Best as it is

Journal Writing Ideas

- What do you like most about November?
- Think about watching a parade. Write about what you see in the parade.

Tennessee Topics

Monday

1 **Which sentence is written correctly?**

- Ⓐ I loves going to the library!
- Ⓑ I uses the computer to find books.
- Ⓒ Sometimes I takes home DVDs.
- Ⓓ I read a library book every week.

Tuesday

2 **Decide which punctuation mark, if any, is needed in the sentence.**

Today I chose a book called *The Story of Davy Crockett*

.	?	!	None
Ⓕ	Ⓖ	Ⓗ	Ⓙ

Wednesday

3 **Read the sentence and decide which part, if any, needs a capital letter.**

Tennessee has | more than 10 million | library books. | None

     Ⓐ   Ⓑ   Ⓒ   Ⓓ

Tennessee Topics

There are a few mistakes in
the sign that need
correcting.

> Welcome to Cedar Lake Public Library!
>
> Today the author James p. Martin
> will speak at 2:00.
>
> He has written books for children.
> He has written books for adults.

Thursday

4 **Choose the <u>best</u> way to write Number 1 in the sign.**

- Ⓕ Today the Author James p. Martin will speak at 2:00.
- Ⓖ Today the author James P. Martin will speak at 2:00.
- Ⓗ Today the author James P. Martin will Speak at 2:00.
- Ⓙ Correct as it is

Friday

5 **What is the <u>best</u> way to combine the sentences in Number 2 in the sign?**

- Ⓐ He has written books for children, and he has written books for adults.
- Ⓑ He has written books for children and has also written books for adults.
- Ⓒ He has written books for children and adults.
- Ⓓ Books for children and adults have been written by him.

Journal Writing Ideas

- Who is an author you enjoy reading? Why?
- Write about a book you like. Tell why you like it.

Tennessee Topics

Monday

1 **Which sentence is written correctly?**

- (A) Morris Frank grown up in Nashville.
- (B) He become blind at the age of 16.
- (C) Frank done something great in Nashville.
- (D) He began a school for guide dogs there.

Tuesday

2 **Which sentence has the correct capitalization and punctuation?**

- (F) America had no guide dogs eighty years ago
- (G) Morris Frank brought a guide dog from Europe.
- (H) the dog's name was Buddy Fortunate Fields.
- (J) Buddy went everywhere with Morris?

Wednesday

3 **Read the sentence and decide which part, if any, needs a capital letter.**

Buddy became | the first guide dog | in america. | None
    (A)   (B)   (C)   (D)

Tennessee Topics

Thursday

4 **Frank named his school The Seeing Eye it still helps people today.** is a run-on sentence. How could it be rewritten to make complete and correctly written sentences?

(F) Frank named his school The Seeing Eye it still helps. People today.

(G) Frank named his school. The Seeing Eye. It still helps people today.

(H) Frank named his school The Seeing Eye. It still helps people today.

(J) Frank named his school, The Seeing Eye it still helps people today.

Friday

5 **Decide which punctuation mark, if any, is needed in the sentence.**

In what city was America's first guide dog school started

    .   **?**   **!**   None

    (A)   (B)   (C)   (D)

Journal Writing Ideas

- Service dogs can be trained to help people in many ways. For example, they can be trained to help guide people who can't see, to alert people who can't hear when sounds occur, or to help people who have seizures. What qualities do dogs possess that make them so useful as service dogs?

- Dogs can be trained to do obey specific commands. What commands would you teach a dog?

Tennessee Topics

Monday

1 **Find the sentence that is complete and written correctly.**

- Ⓐ Grandma and I don't like winter.
- Ⓑ Cold here in Tennessee.
- Ⓒ Cutting wood to stay warm.
- Ⓓ These gloves from Grandma.

Tuesday

2 **Read the sentence and decide which part, if any, needs a capital letter.**

Does the creek | ever freeze | in december? | None

     Ⓕ   Ⓖ   Ⓗ   Ⓙ

Wednesday

3 **Which sentence is written correctly?**

- Ⓐ This was the most coldest winter I remember.
- Ⓑ It was colder than last winter.
- Ⓒ We shoveled most snow than ever!
- Ⓓ The snow is beautifuller than you can imagine.

Tennessee Topics

There are a few mistakes in the sign that need correcting.

> Welcome to Cherokee Lake!
>
> Cherokee Lake is closed for skating. Cherokee Lake is closed for swimming.
>
> Fishing is allowed Friday Saturday, and Sunday.

Thursday

4 **What is the <u>best</u> way to combine the sentences in Number 1 in the sign?**

  Ⓕ Cherokee Lake is closed for skating, and Cherokee Lake is closed for swimming.

  Ⓖ Closed for skating and closed for swimming.

  Ⓗ Cherokee Lake is closed for skating and swimming.

  Ⓙ Cherokee Lake for skating and swimming is closed.

Friday

5 **Choose the <u>best</u> way to write Number 2 in the sign.**

  Ⓐ Fishing is allowed Friday, Saturday, and Sunday.

  Ⓑ Fishing is allowed Friday Saturday and Sunday.

  Ⓒ Fishing is allowed Friday. Saturday, and Sunday.

  Ⓓ Best as it is

Journal Writing Ideas

- What are your favorite things to do in winter?

- Write steps you would follow to make hot chocolate.

Tennessee Topics

Monday

1 **Read the sentence and decide which part, if any, needs a capital letter.**

Josh's favorite park | in Tennessee | is on Cove lake. | None

Ⓐ   Ⓑ   Ⓒ   Ⓓ

Tuesday

2 **Which sentence is written correctly?**

Ⓕ Josh will turn eight on june 11, 2011.

Ⓖ Josh will turn eight on June 11 2011.

Ⓗ Josh will turn eight on june 11 2011.

Ⓙ Josh will turn eight on June 11, 2011.

Wednesday

3 **Find the sentence that is complete and written correctly.**

Ⓐ A picnic birthday party for Josh.

Ⓑ Cooking hotdogs and hamburgers on a grill.

Ⓒ We'll go swimming in the lake.

Ⓓ At one of Tennessee's great parks.

Tennessee Topics

There are a few mistakes in the party invitation that need correcting.

> **1** We having a surprise party for Josh!
>
> **2** Time: saturday, June 11 at Noon
>
> Place: Cove Lake State Park (picnic shelter near the playground)

Thursday

4 Choose the <u>best</u> way to write Number 1 in the invitation.

Ⓕ We is having a surprise party for Josh!

Ⓖ We be having a surprise party for Josh!

Ⓗ We are having a surprise party for Josh!

Ⓙ Correct as it is.

Friday

5 Choose the <u>best</u> way to write part of Number 2 in the invitation

Ⓐ saturday, June 11 at Noon

Ⓑ Saturday, June 11 at noon

Ⓒ Cove lake state park (picnic shelter near the playground)

Ⓓ Cove Lake State park (Picnic Shelter near the playground)

Journal Writing Ideas

• Write about something fun you did at a party.

• Pretend you are planning the perfect birthday party. Where would it be? What would you do?

Tennessee Topics

Monday

1 **Read the sentence and decide which part, if any, needs a capital letter.**

Many battles | of the Civil War | took place in tennessee. | None
   Ⓐ   Ⓑ   Ⓒ   Ⓓ

Tuesday

2 **Decide which punctuation mark, if any, is needed in the sentence.**

The Battle of Nashville was in December of 1864.

  .   ?   !   None
 Ⓕ   Ⓖ   Ⓗ   Ⓙ

Wednesday

3 <u>**Union troops**</u> **is not a complete sentence. Which words could be added to make it a complete and correctly written sentence?**

Union troops _____.

  Ⓐ   took over the city early in the war

  Ⓑ   taking over the city early in the war

  Ⓒ   the city early in the war

  Ⓓ   over the city early in the war

Tennessee Topics

Thursday

4 <u>Some Tennessee soldiers fought for the North some fought for the South.</u> **is a run-on sentence. How could it be rewritten to make complete and correctly written sentences?**

F Some Tennessee soldiers fought. For the North. Some fought for the South.

G Some Tennessee soldiers fought for the North. Some fought for the South.

H Some Tennessee soldiers fought for the North. Some fought. For the South.

J Some Tennessee soldiers. Fought for the North some fought for the South.

Friday

5 Which sentence has the correct capitalization and punctuation?

A There were many Civil War battles in tennessee.

B Some people act out battles.

C This helps others learn about history

D I would like to see something like that?

Journal Writing Ideas

- Write about a place in your town that is famous.

- Write about an important event in history.

© Houghton Mifflin Harcourt Publishing Company

Tennessee Topics

Monday

1 **Read the two sentences.**

Marbles tournaments are fun events.

Marbles tournaments are exciting events.

What is the <u>best</u> way to combine these sentences?

Ⓐ Marbles tournaments are fun events, and marbles tournaments are exciting events.

Ⓑ Marbles tournaments are fun events, and they are also exciting events.

Ⓒ Marbles tournaments are events that are fun and exciting.

Ⓓ Marbles tournaments are fun and exciting events.

Tuesday

2 **Read the sentence and decide which part, if any, needs a capital letter.**

In September, | marbles fans gather | at a state park. | None

    Ⓕ   Ⓖ   Ⓗ   Ⓙ

Wednesday

3 **<u>A big marbles tournament</u> is not a complete sentence. Which words would be added to make it a complete and correctly written sentence?**

A big marbles tournament _____.

Ⓐ every year in Tennessee

Ⓑ at Standing Stone State Park

Ⓒ brings the world's best players

Ⓓ plus music and games for everyone

Tennessee Topics

Thursday

4 Decide which punctuation mark, if any, is needed in the sentence.

Do you know how to make clay marbles

.	?	!	None
Ⓕ	Ⓖ	Ⓗ	Ⓙ

Friday

5 Choose the **best** way to write this sentence.

This stone marble is more older than that glass one.

Ⓐ This stone marble is oldest than that glass one.

Ⓑ This stone marble is most old than that glass one.

Ⓒ This stone marble is older than that glass one.

Ⓓ Best as it is

Journal Writing Ideas

- What type of games do you like to play? Why do you like to play them?

- Tell about a contest or tournament you have been in or seen.

Tennessee Topics

Monday

1 **Find the sentence that is complete and written correctly.**

Ⓐ The first day of the new year.

Ⓑ Put the wrong year on my paper.

Ⓒ It takes some time before I get it right.

Ⓓ Making the same mistake.

Tuesday

2 **Read the sentence and decide which part, if any, needs a capital letter.**

January often brings | snow and ice to | the mountains. | None

     Ⓕ   Ⓖ   Ⓗ   Ⓙ

Wednesday

3 **Which sentence is written correctly?**

Ⓐ The Unaka Mountains is beautiful.

Ⓑ My family goed there for a week.

Ⓒ I seen a pond from the window.

Ⓓ A tall tree grew right by the pond.

Tennessee Topics

There are a few mistakes in the invitation that need correcting.

Celebrate at Clingmans Dome.

 Please join us for a hike. Please join us for party.

 Cake ice cream and cocoa will be served.

Thursday

4 **What is the <u>best</u> way to combine the sentences in Number 1 in the sign?**

Ⓕ Please join us for a hike, and please join us for a party.

Ⓖ Please join us for a hike and join us for a party.

Ⓗ Please join us for a hike and a party.

Ⓙ Please hike and party.

Friday

5 **Choose the <u>best</u> way to write Number 2 in the sign.**

Ⓐ Cake, ice cream, and cocoa will be served.

Ⓑ Cake ice cream, and cocoa will be served.

Ⓒ Cake, ice cream, and cocoa, will be served.

Ⓓ Best as it is

Journal Writing Ideas

• What do you like best about winter?

• What indoor activities do you like to do in winter?

Tennessee Topics   Week 18

Monday

1 **Read the sentence and decide which part, if any, needs a capital letter.**

We just moved | to newport, | Tennessee. | None
    Ⓐ   Ⓑ   Ⓒ   Ⓓ

Tuesday

2 **Decide which punctuation mark, if any, is needed in the sentence.**

Ms. Edwards is my new teacher

   .   ?   !   None
  Ⓕ   Ⓖ   Ⓗ   Ⓙ

Wednesday

3 **Choose the <u>best</u> way to write this sentence.**

My new classmates is friendly.

- Ⓐ My new classmates are friendly.
- Ⓑ My new classmates was friendly.
- Ⓒ My new classmates being friendly.
- Ⓓ Best as it is

Tennessee Topics

Thursday

4 **My teacher is nice her name is Mrs. Brown.** is a run-on sentence. How could it be rewritten to make complete and correctly written sentences?

Ⓔ My teacher is nice her name is. Mrs. Brown.

Ⓖ My teacher. Is nice her name is Mrs. Brown.

Ⓗ My teacher is nice. Her name is Mrs. Brown.

Ⓘ My teacher is nice. Her name. Is Mrs. Brown.

Friday

5 Which sentence is written correctly?

Ⓐ James, Becky, and Alex sits in front of me.

Ⓑ We have gym on Monday, Wednesday, and Friday.

Ⓒ I likes reading, math, and spelling.

Ⓓ Our school have a gym and an art room.

Journal Writing Ideas

- Write about how you would feel in a new place where you did **not** know anyone.

- Write about what makes someone a good friend.

Tennessee Topics

Monday

1 **Which sentence is written correctly?**

Ⓐ   The circus are coming to Nashville, Tennessee.

Ⓑ   The first show are on January 19.

Ⓒ   We wants to go Friday, Saturday, or Sunday.

Ⓓ   Sandy, Tom, and I cannot go on Monday.

Tuesday

2 **Read the two sentences.**

I will see animals at the circus.

I will see clowns at the circus.

What is the <u>best</u> way to combine this sentences?

Ⓕ   I will see animals, and I will see clowns at the circus.

Ⓖ   At the circus, I will see animals and I will see clowns.

Ⓗ   I will see animals and clowns at the circus.

Ⓙ   I will see animals at the circus, and I will see clowns at the circus.

Wednesday

3 **Decide which punctuation mark, if any, is needed in the sentence.**

Have you ever been to the circus

.	?	!	None
Ⓐ	Ⓑ	Ⓒ	Ⓓ

Tennessee Topics   Week 19 (continued)

Thursday

4 <u>With my brother.</u> is not a complete sentence. Which words could be added to make it a complete and correctly written sentence?

_____ with my brother.

- Ⓕ I will go to the circus
- Ⓖ To the circus
- Ⓗ I will the circus
- Ⓙ Going to the circus

Friday

5 Read the sentence and decide which part, if any, needs a capital letter.

my grandparents │ are taking us │ to the circus. │ None

  Ⓐ   Ⓑ   Ⓒ   Ⓓ

Journal Writing Ideas

- Have you ever heard a speech? Write about it.
- Write about going to the circus.

Tennessee Topics   Week 20

Monday

1 **Read the sentence and decide which part, if any, needs a capital letter.**

My friend wrote to | a museum in | chattanooga, Tennessee. | None
   (A)   (B)   (C)   (D)

Tuesday

2 **Which sentence is written correctly?**

  (F)   We goed to the Hunter Museum of Art.

  (G)   The museum are on the Tennessee River.

  (H)   The river are taking sudden turns.

  (J)   Jason leaned over the rail to see a boat.

Wednesday

3 **Find the sentence that is complete and written correctly.**

  (A)   Slipped and scraped his knee.

  (B)   Bandaged his knee.

  (C)   Proud of his bandage.

  (D)   He bandaged his scraped knee.

Tennessee Topics

There are a few mistakes in the letter that need correcting.

 Dear Mr. Lee,

We are taking a class trip.

 We will see statues in the museum.

We will see paintings in the museum.

Please return this form by Friday.

> Sincerely,
>
> Ms. Brody
> Third Grade Teacher

Thursday

4 **Choose the __best__ way to write part of Number 1 in the letter.**

   Ⓕ Dear mr. Lee,   Ⓗ Dear Mr Lee,

   Ⓖ dear mr. Lee,   Ⓙ Best as it is

Friday

5 **What is the __best__ way to combine the sentences in Number 2 in the letter?**

   Ⓐ We will see statues in the museum, and we will see paintings in the museum.

   Ⓑ We will see statues and paintings in the museum.

   Ⓒ We will see statues in the museum and we will see paintings.

   Ⓓ We will see statues and paintings.

Journal Writing Ideas

- Write a letter and describe an adventure you had.
- Write about a time when you were hurt.

Tennessee Topics

Monday

1 **Which sentence is written correctly?**

Ⓐ There is many things you can do on a sunny day.

Ⓑ I likes to swim in the lake.

Ⓒ You can go to the zoo or a ball game.

Ⓓ They wants to go on a picnic.

Tuesday

2 **Read the sentence and decide which part, if any, needs a capital letter.**

Have you ever | been to the | zoo in Memphis? | None

　　　Ⓕ　　　　Ⓖ　　　　　Ⓗ　　　　Ⓙ

Wednesday

3 **Find the sentence that is complete and written correctly.**

Ⓐ Roy and I saw a big bear at the zoo.

Ⓑ Also saw a giraffe with spots.

Ⓒ Is such a fun place.

Ⓓ Were able to stay all day.

Tennessee Topics

Thursday

4 **Choose the <u>best</u> way to write this sentence.**

Everyone like watching the trainers feed the seals.

- Ⓕ Everyone liking watching the trainers feed the seals.
- Ⓖ Everyone is liked watching the trainers feed the seals.
- Ⓗ Everyone likes watching the trainers feed the seals.
- Ⓙ Best as it is

Friday

5 <u>Here is another fun thing to do we can see the Memphis Redbirds.</u> **is a run-on sentence. How could it be rewritten to make complete and correctly written sentences?**

- Ⓐ Here is another fun thing to do. We can see. The Memphis Redbirds.
- Ⓑ Here is another fun thing to do. We can see the Memphis Redbirds.
- Ⓒ Here is another fun thing to do we can see. The Memphis Redbirds.
- Ⓓ Here is another. Fun thing to do we can see the Memphis Redbirds.

Journal Writing Ideas

- Write about what you might see at a zoo.
- Describe what a perfect picnic would be like.

Tennessee Topics

Monday

1 **Decide which punctuation mark, if any, is needed in the sentence.**

Valentine's Day is on February 14

.	?	!	None
Ⓐ	Ⓑ	Ⓒ	Ⓓ

Tuesday

2 **Which sentence is written correctly?**

Ⓕ   My class are having a Valentine's Day food drive.

Ⓖ   We is collecting canned goods.

Ⓗ   The canned goods are being donated.

Ⓙ   We gives them to the Chattanooga Area Food Bank.

Wednesday

3 **Read the sentence and decide which part, if any, needs a capital letter.**

I hope | the food drive | is a success. | None

Ⓐ	Ⓑ	Ⓒ	Ⓓ

Tennessee Topics

Thursday

4 <u>Food drives</u> **is not a complete sentence. Which words could be added to make it a complete and correctly written sentence?**

Food drives _____.

  Ⓕ   be fun

  Ⓖ   fun

  Ⓗ   is fun

  Ⓙ   are fun

Friday

5 **Choose the <u>best</u> way to write this sentence.**

My class helping the community.

  Ⓐ   My class is helping the community.

  Ⓑ   My class be helping the community.

  Ⓒ   My class are helping the community.

  Ⓓ   Correct as it is

Journal Writing Ideas

- Write a poem for a valentine. Your poem can be sweet or silly.

- Do you like to make valentines? Explain how to make one.

© Houghton Mifflin Harcourt Publishing Company

Tennessee Topics

Week 23

Monday

1 **Decide which punctuation mark, if any, is needed in the sentence.**

What holiday is on the third Monday in February

  .   ?   !   None
  Ⓐ Ⓑ Ⓒ   Ⓓ

Tuesday

2 **Find the sentence that is complete and written correctly.**

 Ⓕ Presidents' Day for Lincoln and Washington.

 Ⓖ Always on a Monday.

 Ⓗ I think it's a national holiday.

 Ⓙ Schools closed that day?

Wednesday

3 **Read the sentence and decide which part, if any, needs a capital letter.**

We saw the | tennessee Vols | play basketball. | None
  Ⓐ   Ⓑ   Ⓒ   Ⓓ

Tennessee Topics

There are a few mistakes in the sign that need correcting.

 1   Mark valentine's Day on your calendar!
The Tennessee Vols basketball game is at noon.

 2   Come watch the Tennessee Vols!
Come cheer for the Tennessee Vols!

Thursday

4 Choose the <u>best</u> way to write part of Number 1 in the sign.

Ⓕ   Mark Valentine's Day on your Calendar!

Ⓖ   Mark Valentine's Day on your calendar!

Ⓗ   mark valentine's day on your calendar!

Ⓙ   Correct as it is

Friday

5 What is the <u>best</u> way to combine the sentence in Number 2 in the sign?

Ⓐ   Come watch and cheer for the Tennessee Vols!

Ⓑ   Come watch the Tennessee Vols, and come cheer for the Tennessee Vols!

Ⓒ   Come watch the Tennessee Vols, and cheer!

Ⓓ   Watch the Tennessee Vols and come cheer for the Tennessee Vols!

Journal Writing Ideas

- Describe a sport you like to play. Tell why you like it.

- Write about a holiday that is special to you.

Tennessee Topics   Week 24

Monday

1 Decide which punctuation mark, if any, is needed in the sentence.

Who was Casey Jones

.   ?   !   None

Ⓐ   Ⓑ   Ⓒ   Ⓓ

Tuesday

2 Read the two sentences.

Casey Jones lived in Jackson.

Casey Jones worked for the railroad.

What is the best way to combine these sentences?

Ⓕ   Casey Jones lived in Jackson, and Casey Jones worked for the railroad.

Ⓖ   Casey Jones lived in Jackson, worked for the railroad.

Ⓗ   Casey Jones lived in Jackson and worked for the railroad.

Ⓙ   Casey Jones lived and worked in Jackson for the railroad.

Wednesday

3 Which sentence is written correctly?

Ⓐ   Casey Jones wasn't no fictional character.

Ⓑ   He was a real person and a real hero, two.

Ⓒ   He died in a train crash.

Ⓓ   He were trying to slow the train down.

Tennessee Topics

Thursday

4 <u>Casey Jones</u> is not a complete sentence. Which words could be added to make it a complete and correctly written sentence?

Casey Jones _____.

- Ⓕ   a brave man
- Ⓖ   staying on the train
- Ⓗ   with his hand on the brake
- Ⓙ   saved the lives of his passengers

Friday

5 Find the sentence that is complete and written correctly.

- Ⓐ   Songs about Casey Jones.
- Ⓑ   Casey Jones Home and Railroad Museum.
- Ⓒ   He is a Tennessee hero.
- Ⓓ   Died on April 30, 1900.

Journal Writing Ideas

- Write about someone you think is brave. Why do you think so?
- Who do you consider a hero? What makes that person a hero?

Tennessee Topics

Monday

1 **Read the sentence and decide which part, if any, needs a capital letter.**

last May | I biked | on the Natchez Trace Parkway. | None
  Ⓐ   Ⓑ   Ⓒ   Ⓓ

Tuesday

2 **Decide which punctuation mark, if any, is needed in the sentence.**

My mom and I follow the rules for safe biking

  .   ?   !   None
 Ⓕ   Ⓖ   Ⓗ   Ⓙ

Wednesday

3 **Find the sentence that is complete and written correctly.**

Ⓐ Biking only in daylight hours.

Ⓑ Away from busy roads.

Ⓒ You must wear a helmet.

Ⓓ Hand signals for right and left turns.

Tennessee Topics

There are a few mistakes in the sign that need correcting.

Natchez Trace Parkway

 The Parkway is 444 miles long. The Parkway goes through three states.

 Visitors can camp hike and bike at he Parkway.

Thursday

4 **What is the best way to combine the sentences in Number 1 in the sign?**

Ⓤ The Parkway is 444 miles long, goes through three states.

Ⓠ The Parkway is 444 miles long, and the Parkway goes through three states.

Ⓢ The Parkway is 444 miles long and through three states.

Ⓦ The Parkway is 444 miles long and goes through three states.

Friday

5 **Choose the best way to write Number 2 in the sign.**

Ⓐ Visitors can camp hike, and bike at the Parkway.

Ⓑ Visitors can camp, hike, and bike at the Parkway.

Ⓒ Visitors can, camp, hike, and bike at the Parkway.

Ⓓ Correct as it is

Journal Writing Ideas

- Write about what learning to ride a bike is like.
- Why is it important to follow rules when riding a bike?

Tennessee Topics

Week 26

Monday

1 Find the sentence that is complete and written correctly.

- Ⓐ Found a book about a big battle.
- Ⓑ I read a book about the Civil War.
- Ⓒ Have been watching a show.
- Ⓓ A very interesting show about the Civil War.

Tuesday

2 Read the sentence and decide which part, if any, needs a capital letter.

A big battle | was at the Carter | House in tennessee. | None
    Ⓕ   Ⓖ   Ⓗ   Ⓙ

Wednesday

3 Which sentence is written correctly?

- Ⓐ Zack wants to go there this spring.
- Ⓑ Zack hope to go before it is too hot.
- Ⓒ Zack and I plans to take a picnic.
- Ⓓ The neighbors says they want to come.

Tennessee Topics

There are a few mistakes in the sign that need correcting.

> The Carter House
>
> 1140 Columbus Avenue
>
> Franklin, tennessee
>
> Visit the Carter House to learn about the Battle of Franklin that took place on November, 30, 1864.

Thursday

4 **Choose the <u>best</u> way to write Number 1 in the sign.**

- Ⓕ franklin, tennessee
- Ⓖ Franklin, Tennessee
- Ⓗ Franklin Tennessee
- Ⓙ Correct as it is

Friday

5 **Choose the <u>best</u> way to write part of Number 2 in the sign.**

- Ⓐ November 30, 1864.
- Ⓑ November 30 1864.
- Ⓒ November, 30 1864.
- Ⓓ Correct as it is

Journal Writing Ideas

- Have you ever visited a museum? What was it like?
- What is your favorite book? Why is it your favorite?

Tennessee Topics

Monday

1 **Which sentence is written correctly?**

Ⓐ I has the same birthday as a famous person.

Ⓑ Do you knows who it is?

Ⓒ It is nobody that are still alive.

Ⓓ It is one of the presidents.

Tuesday

2 **Read the sentence and decide which part, if any, needs a capital letter.**

Andrew Jackson | and i were both | born on March 15. | None

   Ⓕ   Ⓖ   Ⓗ   Ⓙ

Wednesday

3 **Decide which punctuation mark, if any, is needed in the sentence.**

Can you guess who was born first

   .   ?   !   None

  Ⓐ   Ⓑ   Ⓒ   Ⓓ

Tennessee Topics

Thursday

4 **Choose the <u>best</u> way to write this sentence.**

Jackson have been our seventh president.

- Ⓕ   Jackson were our seventh president.
- Ⓖ   Jackson was our seventh president.
- Ⓗ   Jackson been our seventh president.
- Ⓙ   Best as it is

Friday

5 **Find the sentence that is complete and written correctly.**

- Ⓐ   Jackson was called Old Hickory.
- Ⓑ   Came from Tennessee.
- Ⓒ   Lived at the Hermitage.
- Ⓓ   The Hermitage near Nashville.

Journal Writing Ideas

- •   What famous person would you like to know more about? What interests you about this person?

- •   Write about a birthday party that you have been to.

Tennessee Topics

Monday

1 **Read the sentence and decide which part, if any, needs a capital letter.**

Would you like | me to set the table | for dinner? | None

    Ⓐ   Ⓑ   Ⓒ   Ⓓ

Tuesday

2 **Find the sentence that is complete and written correctly.**

  Ⓕ   Please put out knives, forks, and spoons.

  Ⓖ   Likes breakfast, lunch, or dinner best?

  Ⓗ   After you eat breakfast.

  Ⓙ   My other chore before we eat.

Wednesday

3 **We finished our chores now we can go have fun. is a run-on sentence. How could it be rewritten to make complete and correctly written sentences?**

  Ⓐ   We finished our chores now we. Can go have fun.

  Ⓑ   We finished. Our chores now we can go have fun.

  Ⓒ   We finished our chores. Now we can go have fun.

  Ⓓ   We finished. Our chores now. We can go have fun.

Tennessee Topics

Thursday

4 **Read the two sentences.**

Ted visited the toy museum in Nashville.

Ted visited the zoo in Nashville.

What is the best way to combine these sentences?

   ⓕ   Ted visited the toy museum and zoo in Nashville.

   ⓖ   The toy museum and a zoo in Nashville, Ted visited.

   ⓗ   Ted visited the toy museum in Nashville and the zoo.

   ⓙ   Ted visited the toy museum in Nashville, and Ted visited the zoo in Nashville.

Friday

5 **A colorful hot-air balloon is not a complete sentence. Which words could be added to make it a complete and correctly written sentence?**

A colorful hot-air balloon _____.

   Ⓐ   passed overhead

   Ⓑ   passing overhead

   Ⓒ   pass overhead

   Ⓓ   were passing overhead

Journal Writing Ideas

- What kinds of chores do you do at home?

- Pretend that you are in a hot-air balloon. What do you see below you?

Tennessee Topics   Week 29

Monday

1 **Read the sentence and decide which part, if any, needs a capital letter.**

The first day │ of spring │ is in march. │ None

　　Ⓐ　　　　　　Ⓑ　　　　　　Ⓒ　　　　　Ⓓ

Tuesday

2 **Decide which punctuation mark, if any, is needed in the sentence.**

How beautiful the Smoky Mountains are in early spring

　　.　　　?　　　!　　　None

　　Ⓕ　　Ⓖ　　Ⓗ　　　Ⓙ

Wednesday

3 **Which sentence is written correctly?**

Ⓐ　Spring flowers blooms in the Smokies.

Ⓑ　I likes the one called spring-beauty.

Ⓒ　Its pink-and-white petals looks pretty.

Ⓓ　They open only when the sun shines.

Tennessee Topics

Thursday

4 Find the sentence that is complete and written correctly.

- Ⓕ Flowers in Smoky Mountains National Park.
- Ⓖ You can see over 1,600 different kinds.
- Ⓗ Dotting the woods with rainbow colors.
- Ⓙ More than in any other park in America.

Friday

5 **I saw some white flowers they looked like snowflakes.** is a run-on sentence. How could it be rewritten to make complete and correctly written sentences?

- Ⓐ I saw some. White flowers they looked. Like snowflakes.
- Ⓑ I saw some white flowers they looked. Like snowflakes.
- Ⓒ I saw some white flowers. They looked like snowflakes.
- Ⓓ I saw. Some white flowers. They looked like snowflakes.

Journal Writing Ideas

- Write about your favorite season. What is it like? What do you like to do?

- Describe something beautiful you have seen in nature.

Tennessee Topics

Monday

1 **Choose the best way to write this sentence.**

Many people enjoys basketball.

- Ⓐ Many people enjoying basketball.
- Ⓑ Many people enjoy basketball.
- Ⓒ Many people is enjoying basketball.
- Ⓓ Correct as it is

Tuesday

2 **Read the two sentences.**

Kayla watches basketball with her dad.

Kayla shoots baskets with her dad.

What is the best way to combine these sentences?

- Ⓕ Kayla watches basketball with her dad, and Kayla shoots baskets with her dad.
- Ⓖ Kayla watches basketball with her dad and shoots baskets with her dad.
- Ⓗ Kayla watches basketball and shoots baskets with her dad.
- Ⓙ Kayla watches basketball with her dad, shoots baskets with her dad.

Wednesday

3 **Kayla's sports hero is not a complete sentence. Which words could be added to make it a complete and correctly written sentence?**

Kayla's sports hero _____.

- Ⓐ was a women's basketball star
- Ⓑ Nera White, a great athlete
- Ⓒ from Macon County, Tennessee
- Ⓓ in the Basketball Hall of Fame

Tennessee Topics

Thursday

4 **Find the sentence that is complete and written correctly.**

- Ⓕ Named most valuable player many times.
- Ⓖ Member of all-star teams.
- Ⓗ Gold medal in the World Basketball Championship in 1957.
- Ⓙ Nera White played in the 1950s and 1960s.

Friday

5 **Decide which punctuation mark, if any, is needed in the sentence.**

What is your favorite sport

.	?	!	None
Ⓐ	Ⓑ	Ⓒ	Ⓓ

Journal Writing Ideas

- Think of a sport that you know about. What skills must someone learn to do this sport well?
- What is your favorite sport? Why?

Tennessee Topics

Monday

1 **Find the sentence that is complete and written correctly.**

- (A) I was reading a very good book.
- (B) Have to stop reading at bedtime.
- (C) Didn't want to turn the light out.
- (D) Could have read all night!

Tuesday

2 **Read the sentence and decide which part, if any, needs a capital letter.**

I read | Tennessee's Presidents | by Frank B. williams. | None

  (F)   (G)   (H)   (J)

Wednesday

3 **Which sentence is written correctly?**

- (A) Jim tell me to go fly a kite.
- (B) I thinks I'd like that.
- (C) Kite flying is fun on a spring day.
- (D) Toby and Sam likes to fly kites.

Tennessee Topics

There are a few mistakes in the sign that need correcting.

> Centennial Park
> nashville, Tennessee
> Please do not play ball on the grass.
> You may picnic on the grass. You may fly kites on the grass.
> Please do not pick the flowers.

Thursday

4 Choose the **best** way to write Number 1 in the sign.

- Ⓕ Nashville, tennessee
- Ⓖ Nashville Tennessee
- Ⓗ Nashville, Tennessee
- Ⓙ Correct as it is

Friday

5 What is the **best** way to combine the sentences in Number 2 in the sign?

- Ⓐ On the grass you may picnic, you may fly kites.
- Ⓑ On the grass for picnics and fly kites.
- Ⓒ You may picnic on the grass, and you may fly kites on the grass.
- Ⓓ You may picnic and fly kites on the grass.

Journal Writing Ideas

- What is it like to fly a kite? Describe this experience.
- Write about a time when you had to do something that you really didn't want to do.

Tennessee Topics

Monday

1 **Which sentence is written correctly?**

- Ⓐ We haved a nature lesson at the pond.
- Ⓑ We seen lots of fish and frogs.
- Ⓒ Some ducks was hiding in the weeds.
- Ⓓ We fed them bread from our lunches.

Tuesday

2 **Our class picture is not a complete sentence. Which words could be added to make it a complete and correctly written sentence?**

Our class picture _____.

- Ⓕ taken at the pond
- Ⓖ was taken at the pond
- Ⓗ at the pond
- Ⓙ taking at the pond

Wednesday

3 **Read the sentence and decide which part, if any, needs a capital letter.**

I was wearing | a shirt i got | in Knoxville. | None

    Ⓐ   Ⓑ   Ⓒ   Ⓓ

Tennessee Topics

Thursday

4 **Choose the <u>best</u> way to write this sentence.**

Many people enjoy hiking near Knoxville.

- Ⓕ Many people enjoys hiking near Knoxville.
- Ⓖ Many people hiking near Knoxville.
- Ⓗ Many people be hiking near Knoxville.
- Ⓙ Best as it is

Friday

5 **Find the sentence that is complete and correctly written.**

- Ⓐ A nature hike in the woods.
- Ⓑ Beautiful orange and yellow butterflies.
- Ⓒ We collected leaves on our hike.
- Ⓓ Climbing up a steep hill.

Journal Writing Ideas

- Write the word *nature* at the top of your page. Explain what this word means to you.

- Think of your favorite photograph of yourself. Describe it, and explain why you like it.

Tennessee Topics

Monday

1 **<u>The third grade went on a field trip we went to Memphis.</u> is a run-on sentence. How could it be rewritten to make complete and correctly written sentences?**

Ⓐ The third grade went on a field trip. We went to Memphis.

Ⓑ The third grade. Went on a field trip we went to Memphis.

Ⓒ The third grade went. On a field trip we went to Memphis.

Ⓓ The third grade went on. A field trip we went to Memphis.

Tuesday

2 **Which sentence is written correctly?**

Ⓕ Our class go on a field trip this spring.

Ⓖ The driver take a wrong turn on the way home.

Ⓗ We gots back to school late.

Ⓙ Our parents were waiting for us.

Wednesday

3 **Decide which punctuation mark, if any, is needed in the sentence.**

Ms. Turner used a map to find the state capital

.	?	!	None
Ⓐ	Ⓑ	Ⓒ	Ⓓ

Tennessee Topics

Thursday

4 Read the sentence and decide which part, if any, needs a capital letter.

Our school is | on elm Street | in Chattanooga. | None

    Ⓕ   Ⓖ   Ⓗ   Ⓙ

Friday

5 Find the sentence that is complete and written correctly.

Ⓐ   I would not be a good bus driver.

Ⓑ   Don't know how to get places.

Ⓒ   All of the noisy children.

Ⓓ   Needs to be on time.

Journal Writing Ideas

- Pretend that you are in charge of planning your next class field trip. Where in Tennessee will you go? What will you do when you get there?

- If you could change one thing about yourself, what would it be?

Tennessee Topics

Week 34

Monday

1 **Read the sentence and decide which part, if any, needs a capital letter.**

My family will | celebrate my birthday | on may 5. | None
(A)   (B)   (C)   (D)

Tuesday

2 **Which sentence is written correctly?**

Ⓕ   We always does something special together.

Ⓖ   This year we am going to the Nashville Zoo.

Ⓗ   My sister want to be a zookeeper.

Ⓙ   She loves all kinds of animals.

Wednesday

3 **Find the sentence that is complete and written correctly.**

Ⓐ   Getting tickets while Mom parks the car.

Ⓑ   Mom will meet us at the gate by the flags.

Ⓒ   The red, white, and blue Tennessee flag.

Ⓓ   A short walk from the parking lot.

Tennessee Topics

There are a few mistakes in the sign that need correcting.

> Welcome to the Nashville Zoo.
> 1 The Animals are fed at noon.
> 2 Please don't tease the animals.
> Please don't feed the animals.

Thursday

4 **Choose the best way to write Number 1 in the sign.**

- Ⓕ The animals are fed at noon?
- Ⓖ The animals are fed at noon.
- Ⓗ the animals are fed at noon
- Ⓗ Best as it is

Friday

5 **What is the best way to combine the sentences in Number 2 in the sign?**

- Ⓐ Please don't tease and don't feed the animals.
- Ⓑ Please don't tease the animals, and please don't feed the animals.
- Ⓒ Please don't tease or feed the animals.
- Ⓓ Please don't tease the animals, but don't feed them.

Journal Writing Ideas

- If you could start your own zoo, what animals would you like to have in it?

- Where would you like to go with your family?

Tennessee Topics

Week 35

Monday

1 Read the sentence and decide which part, if any, needs a capital letter.

we learned many | facts about | Tennessee this year. | None
    Ⓐ   Ⓑ   Ⓒ   Ⓓ

Tuesday

2 Find the sentence that is complete and written correctly.

- Ⓕ Wilma Rudolph played basketball.
- Ⓖ Came from a big family.
- Ⓗ Born in Clarksville, Tennessee.
- Ⓗ Became a famous runner.

Wednesday

3 Decide which punctuation mark, if any, is needed in the sentence.

The Knoxville World Fair opened on May 1, 1982

.   ?   !   None
Ⓐ   Ⓑ   Ⓒ   Ⓓ

Tennessee Topics

Thursday

4 **Choose the best way to write this sentence.**

Jim saying that soccer should be the state sport.

Ⓕ Jim say that soccer should be the state sport.

Ⓖ Jim says that soccer should be the state sport.

Ⓗ Jim sayed that soccer should be the state sport.

Ⓗ Best as it is

Friday

5 **We have two state insects they are the ladybug and the firefly. is a run-on sentence. How could it be rewritten to make complete and correctly written sentences?**

Ⓐ We have two state insects they are. The ladybug and the firefly.

Ⓑ We have two state insects. They are the ladybug and the firefly.

Ⓒ We have two. State insects. They are the ladybug and the firefly.

Ⓓ We have two state insects they. Are the ladybug and the firefly.

Journal Writing Ideas

- What do you think should be the state sport? Why?
- Describe what a ladybug looks like.

Tennessee Topics

Monday

1 **Decide which punctuation mark, if any, is needed in the sentence.**

Do you like listening to stories

.	?	!	None
Ⓐ	Ⓑ	Ⓒ	Ⓓ

Tuesday

2 **Find the sentence that is complete and written correctly.**

- Ⓕ Going to a big storytelling festival.
- Ⓖ In Jonesborough, Tennessee each fall.
- Ⓗ People tell wonderful stories.
- Ⓗ Funny, wise, make-believe, and true stories.

Wednesday

3 **Read the sentence and decide which part, if any, needs a capital letter.**

Is the festival | in September or october | next fall? | None
    Ⓐ   Ⓑ   Ⓒ   Ⓓ

Tennessee Topics

Thursday

4 **Which sentence is written correctly?**

- Ⓕ Many people comes to the storytelling festival.
- Ⓖ They listens to stories in big tents.
- Ⓗ One man tell Choctaw stories.
- Ⓗ My sister likes the funny stories best.

Friday

5 **My three cousins** **is not a complete sentence. Which words could be added to make it a complete and correctly written sentence?**

My three cousins _____.

- Ⓐ to the storytelling festival
- Ⓑ going to the storytelling festival
- Ⓒ will go to the storytelling festival
- Ⓓ is going to the storytelling festival

Journal Writing Ideas

- Think of a story you liked very much. What was it about? Why did you like it? Tell a little about your favorite part.

- Think of a character you remember from a story. Tell about this character.

© Houghton Mifflin Harcourt Publishing Company